PRIORITY
IN
BIBLICAL HERMENEUTICS
AND
THEOLOGICAL METHOD

Christopher Cone, Th.D, Ph.D, Ph.D

EXEGETICA PUBLISHING
2018

Priority in Biblical Hermeneutics and Theological Method
© 2018 Christopher Cone
Published by Exegetica Publishing, Raymore, MO

ISBN-13: 978-0-9982805-2-3
ISBN-10: 0-9982805-2-6

All rights reserved. No part of this publication may be reproduced, stored in a retrieval system, or transmitted in any form or by any means – electronic, mechanical, photocopy, recording, or any other – except for brief quotation in printed reviews, without the prior permission of the publisher.

All Scripture quotations, except those noted otherwise are from the New American Standard Bible, ©1960, 1962, 1963, 1968, 1971, 1972, 1973, 1975, and 1977 by the Lockman Foundation.

CONTENTS

1 PRIORITY OF EPISTEMOLOGICAL QUESTIONS IN DERIVING A WORLDVIEW..1

2 PRIORITY OF INTERCONNECTEDNESS IN PHILOSOPHY, THEOLOGY, AND WORLDVIEW 9

3 PRIORITY IN EPISTEMOLOGICAL INQUIRY OF IDENTIFYING THE SOURCE OF AUTHORITY.................13

4 PRIORITY OF GENESIS FOR UNDERSTANDING THE SOURCE OF AUTHORITY 17

5 PRIORITY OF EPISTEMOLOGICAL FOUNDATIONS IN THEOLOGICAL METHOD..37

6 PRIORITY OF AUTHENTICITY IN THE SOURCE OF AUTHORITY...55

7 PRIORITY OF BIBLICAL HERMENEUTICS OVER THEOLOGICAL SYSTEMS..77

8 PRIORITY OF OLD TESTAMENT LITERALISM IN NEW TESTAMENT USAGE 83

9 PRIORITY OF HERMENEUTICS IN RESOLVING TEXTUAL DIFFICULTIES 107

10 PRIORITY OF HERMENEUTICS IN GENRE DETERMINATIONS: THE GENRE OF GENESIS 1 129

11 PRIORITY OF HERMENEUTICS IN GENRE DETERMINATIONS: THE RESURRECTION AND GRECO-ROMAN BIOS 135

12 PRIORITY OF HERMENEUTICS IN GENRE DETERMINATIONS: REVELATION AND APOCALYPTIC LITERATURE 145

13 PRIORITY OF HERMENEUTICS IN METAPHYSICS: THE HERMENEUTIC ROOTS OF OUR SOTERIOLOGICAL CRISIS 149

14 PRIORITY OF HERMENEUTICS AND THEOLOGICAL METHOD IN METAPHYSICS: THE DISTINCTION BETWEEN ISRAEL AND THE CHURCH 159

15 PRIORITY OF HERMENEUTICS IN APPLICATION AND ETHICS: THE DISJUNCT BETWEEN DESCRIPTIVE AND PRESCRIPTIVE 199

16 PRIORITY OF HERMENEUTICS IN SOCIO – POLITICAL THOUGHT: THE NECESSITY OF PREMILLENNIALISM 205

17 IMPLICATIONS OF PRIORITY IN HERMENEUTICS AND THEOLOGICAL METHOD 235

1
PRIORITY OF EPISTEMOLOGICAL QUESTIONS IN DERIVING A WORLDVIEW

There are four major areas of philosophical inquiry that make up the basic components of worldview: epistemology, metaphysics, ethics, and socio-political philosophy. Epistemology (the study of knowledge) addresses the question of how we can know what is true and what is not. Metaphysics (the study of reality) addresses the question of what exists. Ethics (the study of what should be done) addresses the question of what we should do in light of what reality is. Socio-political philosophy (the study of ethics on a societal scale) addresses the question of how communities and society should behave.

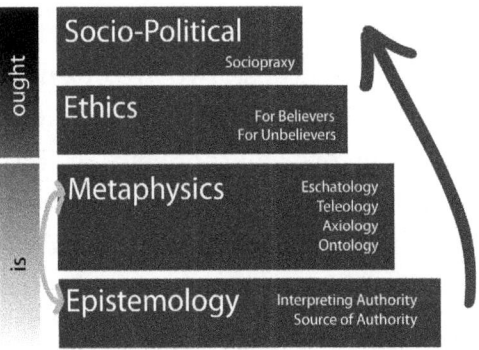

The worldview chart illustrates a logical ordering of these topics of inquiry. The arrow on the far right indicates that we begin at the bottom and move toward the top. We can't address socio-political issues until we deal with ethics, we can't handle ethics until we answer questions of metaphysics, and we can't answer the metaphysics questions until we address the epistemological ones.

The arrow to the left indicates that, in a sense, the ordering of epistemology and metaphysics can be reversed, based on perspective. From the perspective of reality, the metaphysical answers are what they are, regardless of our understanding of them. Reality is what it is, regardless of what you and I think or believe about it. So from the perspective of reality, metaphysics is first. But from the perspective of the inquirer, they must first address the questions of how they can gain knowledge, truth, and certainty, in order to address the metaphysical questions. So, from the perspective of the inquirer, epistemology is the first necessary step in formulating a worldview.

Epistemology is the study of knowledge and seeks to answer the question of how we can have knowledge and certainty. Metaphysics is the study of reality and responds to questions regarding whether there is anything beyond the physical or natural. While these two are often spoken of here as interdependent, I have also been outspoken regarding the priority of epistemology over metaphysics in the context of fields of inquiry. Some might conclude from that prioritization that I am a foundationalist. Foundationalism is a theory of epistemic justification (particularly espoused by Aristotle, and later, Descartes) that demands that beliefs must be warranted, or based on some foundation (in contrast to, for example, coherentism, which simply requires that a belief be coherent with a set of other coherently fitting beliefs in order to be justified). In prioritizing epistemology over metaphysics as a field of inquiry, I am not drawing a foundationalist conclusion, but I am carefully qualifying the *context* of that prioritization.

Clearly, if we are considering the realm of reality, or asking about what actually exists, then metaphysics comes first. Reality comes before the questioning of that reality. What exists, exists, and whether it is questioned or not has no bearing at all on its existence. So, in the realm of what actually is, metaphysics comes first. However, in the context of human inquiry, we are seeking to understand what actually is. Metaphysics cannot come first in this context, because we have to have a reason to prefer one explanation to another.

This is not to draw a foundationalist conclusion, for example, that the existence of God must be justified in order to be true. On the contrary. God's existence has nothing to do with whether or not He can be explained or whether or not His existence is warranted. He either exists or He doesn't. But human inquiry in this area is the pursuit of understanding what is true. Does He exist or doesn't He?

Various epistemological models justify their conclusions in different ways. Humean empiricism says He doesn't exist because He has not been (and presumably cannot be) sensed. Cartesian rationalism reasons to His existence from the first assumption that He doesn't exist. But the Biblical model describes the fear of the Lord as the beginning of wisdom (Prov 1:7, 9:10). Consequently, the Biblical epistemology assumes the Biblical God's existence at the outset and works from that premise. That He exists comes first – that is the metaphysical actuality.

Metaphysically speaking, *that we understand* He exists comes after the fact of the reality. But how we come to understand He exists is the epistemological question that we must first answer before we can *support* the metaphysical supposition and know whether or not that supposition is certain or correct. Metaphysics (the reality) comes first in actuality, but epistemology (how we can answer the question of what is reality) comes first in inquiry. Before we can derive answers in any field of inquiry, we must have some basis for preferring some answers to others. That is the epistemological question. Our preferring some answers to others has no bearing on the actual legitimacy of those answers, but is an important reflection on the source of authority upon which we rely.

For a Biblicist, that source of authority is the Bible. According to the Bible, that God exists is the metaphysical reality (Gen 1:1) – and that comes first in the realm of actuality. At the same time, the Bible also asserts epistemic truth regarding how we can have knowledge and certainty – by the fear of (right perspective of and response to) the Lord (Prov 1:7, 9:10). The epistemic proposition is simply that knowledge begins with the acknowledgment of Him. For the purposes of our inquiry, we are given, as first principle, the means whereby we can have certainty of knowledge. In other words, in the realm of the human pursuit of wisdom and knowledge, the epistemic question comes first (how can we have wisdom and knowledge?), and is answered with metaphysical reality (by the fear of the Lord).

Once we answer the epistemological questions, we can address the metaphysics questions. Once we answer those we can move on to the ethics questions, and then the socio-political ones.

At this point, take notice of the far left column on the worldview chart, which distinguishes between the lower two categories as *is*, from the upper two categories as *ought*. The bottom two categories (epistemology and metaphysics) are descriptive – dealing with what *is*. The top two categories (ethics and socio-political) are considering the prescriptive – addressing what *ought* to be. The is/ought challenge is that in order to move from description (what is) to prescription (what ought to be), that maneuver should be justified within the worldview itself – the *ought* should necessarily follow from the *is*.

From a Biblical perspective, Paul illustrates the is/ought relationship in his letters to the Romans and to the Ephesians. In Romans, he addresses the epistemological and metaphysical questions in chapters 1-11, and in 12:1 he says, "Therefore I urge you, brethren, by the mercies of God, to present your bodies a living and holy sacrifice, acceptable to God, which is your spiritual service of worship." He moves from the *is* of description (describing the mercies of God) to the *ought* of prescription (Therefore...present your bodies...). In Ephesians, he addresses the epistemological and metaphysical questions in the first three chapters, introducing that believers have every spiritual blessing in the heavenlies in Christ (1:3), and then in 4:1 he prescribes, "Therefore I, the prisoner of the Lord, implore you to walk in a manner worthy of the calling with which you have been called..." In both of these examples, the position (the description of reality, the is) leads to the practice (the prescription, the ought). Once an accurate description is established, the prescription can be engaged.

Beginning, then, with epistemology, we have to address two issues. First, we have to identify the source of authority. Every worldview relies on an ultimate source of authority.

Hume's empiricism relies on experience, Descartes' rationalism depends on reason, Nietzsche's existentialism on the individual's existence, and the Biblical model depends on God as revealed in the Bible.

Further, every worldview requires a first, self-authenticating step – a leap of faith, so to speak. Hume demonstrates faith in the human sensory apparatus. Descartes demonstrates faith in the human reasoning apparatus. But these first principles are assumed, rather than provable. To illustrate, consider the late astrophysicist Carl Sagan's opening statement in his bestselling *The Cosmos*: "The Cosmos is all that is or was or ever will be."[1] This is the faith statement, or first principle upon which he builds his worldview. It is circular reasoning, in the sense that it begs several questions, but as a first step, it is a necessary faith step. One common feature of all worldviews is that the first step is a step of faith. The question that ultimately determines the validity or invalidity of a worldview is whether or not that the object of that first step of faith is worthy of that faith.

In the Biblical model, the first step is faith that the Biblical God exists, and that He has revealed Himself (Prov 1:7, 2:6, 9:10). In the Biblical model, we discover that God revealed Himself in three ways: (1) general revelation – in creation (cf. Gen 1 and Rom 1), (2) personal revelation – Jesus Christ is God incarnate, revealed in the flesh (Jn 1, Col 1, Heb 1), and (3) special revelation – in the original autographs of the Biblical text (2 Tim 3:16-17, 1 Pet 1:20-21). God's revelation in nature is sufficient for all to have the knowledge of His invisible attributes, eternal power, and divine nature (Rom 1:20). His

---

[1] Carl Sagan, *The Cosmos* (NY: Ballantine, 1980), 1.

revelation in Jesus Christ allows all to access the Father through the Person and work of the Son (Jn 14:6, 1 Tim 2:5). God's special revelation – the Bible provides that which is necessary for the believer to be equipped for every good work (2 Tim 3:16-17). Notice the correlation, once again, between the descriptions of reality as found in Scripture, and their provision for equipping believers for practice. The epistemology and metaphysics of Scripture provide for ethics and socio-political practice. Simply put, in the Biblical model, God is the source of authority, and our worldview inquiry seeks to understand Him through His revelation in Scripture.

The second key question addressed in epistemology is how to interpret that source of authority. In the case of Hume's empiricism, for example, the hermeneutic (or method of interpretation) for experience is derived through the senses. How does Hume interpret experience? Through the senses. How does Descartes interpret knowledge? Through the guided use of reason. In order for us to maintain a Biblical epistemology we need to find a hermeneutic *in the Bible itself.* If we have to go outside the Bible to answer this important question, then the resulting worldview is not a Biblical one – it is derived from something else. That is the task here: to examine the Biblical model for hermeneutics, understanding the priorities that help guide us in arriving at Biblical conclusions.

As we pursue that quest, we discover that the Bible does provide a hermeneutic model to follow. In the book of Genesis, as detailed in Chapter 4, for example, there are nearly one hundred references to God speaking, and in all the instances where the response is provided in the text, God either interprets Himself, or the other listeners interpret Him in a normative, literal grammatical historical way. Because Genesis covers roughly the first two-thousand years of recorded history, the hermeneutic model provided in the book is broadly indicative of how God expects to be understood. In short, the Bible provides its own hermeneutic model, and thus answers the question of how we are to interpret the Source of authority. Once we answer the key epistemological questions, we can move forward in understanding the Biblical worldview. In the chapters that follow, the focus is on the role of epistemology – and the priority of hermeneutics specifically – in rightly understanding the worldview and theology that is presented in Scripture.

2
PRIORITY OF INTERCONNECTEDNESS IN PHILOSOPHY, THEOLOGY, AND WORLDVIEW

A worldview is the perspective through which one views the world. By definition, a Biblical worldview is derived exegetically from the pages of the Bible. Philosophy and theology have long been perceived as rivals in worldview, but if we define those terms lexically and through a Scriptural lens, then we find no friction between the two disciplines. In fact, the two are complementary.

Philosophy as a discipline is recognized as "the systematic and critical study of fundamental questions that arise both in everyday life and through the practice of other disciplines."[2] Philosophy *the discipline* is often confused with philosophy *as a particular worldview*. The discipline is informed by the worldview (or the perspective by which the philosopher is viewing philosophy), but the discipline is distinct from worldview. For example, many of the early Greek philosophers set out to find answers to life's great questions using *only* naturalistic evidences. To their credit, they were in part motivated by a desire to move away from superstition and

---

[2] "Philosophy: What and Why?, viewed at https://www.brown.edu/academics/philosophy/undergraduate/philosophy-what-and-why.

unwarranted belief in a pantheon that was hardly explanatory. The naturalistic worldview of these thinkers shaped much of what we understand as philosophical inquiry, but it is important to note that it was their worldview that was naturalistic, not the discipline of philosophy itself.

The Apostle Paul cautions against any philosophy that would deceive, and contrasts between philosophy rooted in humanism (or according to the traditions of men) and philosophy rooted in Christ (Col 2:8). Paul's warning illustrates the distinction between a worldview and the discipline. A Biblical philosophy is one that acknowledges Christ's identity (2:9), explanatory value (2:10a), and authority as Creator (2:10b). One inference from Paul's statement is that one's philosophy is correct insofar as it is Christologically correct. For Paul, theology and philosophy are intertwined.

The Biblical worldview applied to philosophy helps us understand philosophy in its lexical sense as the love of wisdom, and points us to the first principles of that wisdom as the proper perspective of and response to God (Prov 1;7, 9:10), and to the source of that wisdom as the word of God (Prov 2:6). As theology is *the study of God*, the theological discipline of Bibliology (the study of the Bible) is paramount at this introductory stage of worldview and philosophy.

The process of doing philosophy includes beginning with answering questions related to how we acquire knowledge, truth, and certainty. These are questions of epistemology. Every worldview (and philosophy) must first identify its source of authority – who or what it will trust to provide knowledge, truth, and certainty. In the Biblical worldview, that source is God revealed through Scripture. Another vital component of epistemological enquiry is how that source of authority is interpreted or understood – *hermeneutics*. Without a proper hermeneutic framework as the capstone to epistemology, it is difficult to find either transparency or consistency in a worldview.

Once the epistemological questions are answered, there is a matrix for addressing the metaphysical questions – those questions pertaining to the nature of reality. Metaphysics considers four major areas: ontology (the nature of existence), axiology (the nature of value), teleology (the nature of design and purpose), and eschatology (the nature of the future). These four areas of study overlap the major categories of theology (Bibliology is not in this list, as it is addressed as part of the inquiry of Epistemology):

- Theology Proper – the study of God the Father
- Christology – the study of Christ
- Pneumatology – the study of the Spirit of God
- Angelology – the study of angels, demons, and the spiritual world
- Natural Theology – the study of nature as substance (natural sciences) and as revelatory device for God's invisible attributes, eternal power, and divine nature (Rom 1:20)
- Anthropology – the study of humanity and everything directly related to human existence (for example, the discipline of psychology would fit in this category)
- Hamartialogy – the study of sin and its impact
- Soteriology – the study of salvation and its impact
- Ecclesiology – the study of the assembly we call the church
- Israelology – the study of the nation of Israel, as unique and chosen, and where it fits in God's plan

- Eschatology – the study of last things, the future, and ultimate fulfillment of Biblical promises

Each of these theological topics fit within the greater discipline of metaphysics, and without attention to each one, an overall metaphysical understanding would be deficient.

Epistemology and Metaphysics provides the *is* of philosophy – the descriptive aspects of reality. Flowing from that *is* there is an *ought*. Ethics provides the *ought* on an individual scale, and socio-political on a societal scale.

In a Biblical worldview, there are two major categories of ethics – one for unbelievers (to become believers), and one for believers (to become more like Christ). Socio-political concepts round out the philosophical discussion, as various distinctives in society are considered, including the nations in general, Israel specifically, the universal church, and local fellowships of the universal church.

A reasonably ordered philosophy, seen from a Biblical perspective, overlaps major theological concepts and provides a broad and comprehensive backdrop for enquiry in any discipline. In a Biblical approach, philosophy and theology are interconnected, and in some cases even interchangeable. This close relationship between the two disciplines of philosophy and theology invites inquisitiveness and pursuit of knowledge in every area, and nothing about the Biblical approach to these disciplines would restrict or de-incentivize learning and discovery. Approaching any discipline from a Biblical worldview perspective invites the enquirer to examine thoroughly, and to "taste and see that the Lord is good" (Ps 34:8).

3
PRIORITY IN EPISTEMOLOGICAL INQUIRY OF IDENTIFYING THE SOURCE OF AUTHORITY

In any worldview there is a necessary first step of establishing the source of authority. Simply put, our first step is a step of faith in determining who or what we will trust in order to answer the questions of life. This is the first task of epistemology. For Hume that source of authority is human experience through the lens of the senses. Hume trusts the sensory abilities as the only trustworthy means of determining truth. Descartes, on the other hand, argues that the senses are less than reliable, and truth must be gathered through a process of reason guided by his method. For Descartes the human apparatus of reason can be harnessed in such a way as to lead us to truth. Nietzsche's model is less reliant on either the senses or reason, and instead trusts the self as the ultimate arbiter of truth. Plato saw limitations of both experience and reason, and considered enlightened learning a better way to come to a true knowledge of reality. His divided line theory provided a model seemingly advantageous to the philosopher in arriving at truth.

These first steps of faith suggested by Plato, Descartes, Hume, and Nietzsche have been broadly received, as they ground prominent worldviews. However, they do not account for the inherent limitations of learning, reason, experience, and perspective (the latter in Nietzsche's case). Consequently, while they each are broadly explanatory, they are not, in my estimation, satisfactorily explanatory in the quest for truth.

The Bible, on the other hand, makes sweeping claims regarding the source of authority. Solomonic epistemology, for example, is grounded on the premise that competing epistemic groundings are vanity (e.g., Ecc 1:1). The pursuit of wisdom and learning, while certainly having practical value, is ultimately futility and striving after wind (Ecc 2:12-17; 7:23-29) and even leads to grief and pain (Ecc 1:12-18). The stimulation of the senses, though temporally rewarding, is vanity, striving after wind, and unprofitable (Ecc 2:1-11). The pursuit of self is inherently limited (Ecc 3:11), cannot aid in what comes after this earthly life (Ecc 6:10-12), and ultimately is characterized more by evil and insanity (Ecc 9:3) than wellbeing and certainty.

Solomon prescribes each of these terrestrial pursuits insofar as they have value, but only if the interlocutor is first willing to acknowledge that these pursuits are not ends in themselves. He advocates pursuing wisdom and learning, but only with the understanding that God will bring every resulting act to judgment (Ecc 12:9-13). Solomon advises the use of reason for its benefits (Ecc 10:10), but acknowledges that its use is limited in comparison to the certainties God possesses (Ecc 11:5). Solomon encourages the stimulation of the senses, but only insofar as they are used in the context of remembering the Creator, because those senses will become increasingly ineffective until ultimately they are silenced in death (Ecc 12:1-8). Finally, Solomon advocates following the impulses of the heart (the self), but only with the admission that God will judge the follower for those pursuits (Ecc 11:9-10).

Solomon answers each epistemological model with the same alternative: a beyond-the-sun worldview provides certainty, whereas an under-the-sun worldview provides none. Simply put, under the sun we do not know the activity of God who makes all things (Ecc 11:5). Consequently, for us to have a worldview grounded in certainty, it must be premised on an acknowledgement of the Creator. Solomon pronounces that records of truth – wisdom and delightful words – are given by one Shepherd (Ecc 12:9-11), and in so stating reveals that God's word is the answer to the epistemological first inquiry regarding what is the source of authority. Elsewhere, Solomon recognizes that the fear of the Lord is the beginning of knowledge (Prov 1:7), the beginning of wisdom, and that the knowledge of the Holy One is understanding (9:10).

Solomon writes so that his readers will know wisdom and instruction and have discernment (Prov 1:1), to instruct them in the fear of the Lord as the source of strong confidence and refuge (Prov 14:26). Consequently he prescribes that humanity must fear God (Ecc 3:14, 5:7, 12:13). And what is the authoritative source from whence we discover the fear of the Lord? Solomon answers this all-important question directly: "Then you will discern the fear of the Lord, and discover the knowledge of God. For the Lord gives wisdom; from His mouth come knowledge and understanding (Prov 2: 5-6). God's word, according to Solomon, is the source of authority whereby we can have certainty.

4

PRIORITY OF GENESIS FOR UNDERSTANDING THE SOURCE OF AUTHORITY: ASCERTAINING BIBLICAL HERMENEUTIC METHOD[3]

Introduction

In order to arrive at a *Scriptural approach* for interpreting Scriptures, the interpretive method must be exegetically derived from within the Scriptural text. Otherwise, there can be no claim to hermeneutic certainty, because any externally derived interpretive method can be preferred and applied simply by exerting presuppositions upon the text. In the case of an externally derived hermeneutic, presuppositions leading to that hermeneutic conclusion create a pre-understanding that predetermines meaning independent of the author's intentions. The outcome, in such a case, can be wildly different than what the author had in mind.

If the Bible is merely a collection of ancient stories, legends, and myth, interspersed with mildly historical accounts, then the stakes are not particularly high. In that case, the greatest damage we can inflict by a faulty hermeneutic method is of the same weight as misunderstanding the motivations and activities of Mark Twain's adventurous character, *Tom Sawyer*,

---

[3] Originally presented as "The Genesis Account as Early Model for Scriptural Hermeneutics," to the Symposium on Scripture, Hermeneutics and Language, San Diego State University, April 13, 2015.

for example. In such an instance we would simply fail to recognize the aesthetic virtues of a creative work. However, if the Bible constitutes an actual revelation from God, then it bears the very authority of the Author, Himself – an authority that extends to every aspect of life and conduct. These are high stakes, indeed. If we fail to engage the text with the interpretive approach intended by its Author, then we fail not just to appreciate aesthetic qualities, but we fail to grasp who God is, and what He intends for us to do.

It is incumbent, then, upon readers of the text to carefully derive hermeneutic method from the Scriptures themselves. Yet, this responsibility is complicated by an obvious absence of prescriptive material within the Biblical text that if present could direct readers toward a particular interpretive stance. In the absence of such prescriptive material, we examine here some descriptive elements from the book of Genesis, in order to discover whether or not there is actually a prevailing hermeneutic embedded in the text itself.

From the opening of Genesis to its conclusion, the book records roughly two thousand years of history. Further, Genesis alleges that these two thousand years are the *first years* of human history (c.f., Gen 1:27 and 5:1). Within that framework of chronology, the events in the book of Genesis account for the first 33% of our recorded six-thousand-year history and the first 50% of the four thousand years of Biblical history. *If Genesis were univocal regarding hermeneutic method*, that single voice would go a long way in helping us understand how the Author intended for us to interpret the Scriptures. Genesis would be a guiding light, providing the time-tested descriptive model foundational to our Scriptural hermeneutics.

In order to assess the hermeneutic method applied *within Genesis, during the times which the book describes*, we simply examine in Genesis the occurrences of God speaking and the responses of those who heard. The questions addressed here include whether or not God's initial audiences took Him *only* literally or whether they instead or additionally perceived that He intended a deeper meaning than what would be normally signified by the words that were verbally expressed. The responses are categorized as follows: Category 1 (C1) responses are those providing evidence that the initial speech act was intended for literal understanding only; category 2 (C2) responses are those providing evidence that the initial speech act was intended for any understanding beyond the literal meaning of the words verbally expressed.

The Speech Acts of God and Responses in Genesis

There are four key phrases that introduce the speech acts of God in Genesis: "God said"[4] (thirty-six verses), "the Lord said"[5] (nineteen verses), "the Lord God said"[6] (five verses), and "He said (twenty-four verses).[7] With only the exception of ten verses in the book of Job, these eighty-four verses constitute all Scripturally recorded instances of God verbally communicating during the first two thousand years of human history. The passages in Job are considered at the conclusion of this paper as

---

[4] Generally, Heb. *wayyomer el* or *wayyomer elohim*.
[5] Generally, Heb *wayyomer yahweh*.
[6] Generally, Heb *wayyomer yahweh elohim*.
[7] The "He said" passages listed here employ the pronoun to instances in which "God," "the Lord," "the Lord God," or in some cases, "the angel of the Lord" were mentioned in near-context verses as the antecedent to the pronoun.

a complement to and confirmation of the hermeneutic evident in Genesis.[8]

God Said (thirty-six verses/ at least twenty-seven C1's)
- Genesis 1:3 – God commands light into existence. Light responds with a C1.
- Genesis 1:6 – God commands an expanse into existence. God responds with a C1 in 1:7, making the expanse.
- Genesis 1:9 – God commands dry land to appear. The dry land responds with a C1.
- Genesis 1:11 – God commands into existence vegetation to function a specific way. Vegetation responds with a C1, both by beginning to exist and by beginning to otherwise function as commanded.
- Genesis 1:14 – God commands into existence heavenly lights to distinguish times and seasons. Heavenly lights respond with a C1, both by beginning to exist and by serving the purpose prescribed.
- Genesis 1:20 – God commands into existence creatures in water and above the earth. Creatures respond with a C1, both by beginning to exist and by functioning as prescribed.
- Genesis 1:24 – God commands into existence creatures on the earth. Creatures respond with a C1, both by beginning to exist and by functioning as prescribed.

---

[8] The events of Job are generally recognized to have taken place during the patriarchal times recorded in Genesis, in part, due to the genealogical information connecting Eliphaz and Jobab (e.g., Gen 36:4, 33; Job 2:11), of the land of Uz.

- Genesis 1:26 – God states His intention to create mankind. God responds in 1:27 with a C1, executing exactly what He had described in 1:26.
- Genesis 1:28 – God commands mankind to multiply and exercise dominion. There is no direct response recorded in the immediate context.
- Genesis 1:29 – God adds explanation to the command of 1:28. There is no direct response in the immediate context.
- Genesis 3:1 – Satan distorts what God said in order to cause Eve to question God's word. Eve responds with a C1 in 3:2-3, as she corrects Satan's misquote
- Genesis 3:3 – Eve responds to Satan's question with a literal, though not entirely correct restatement of God's command. Satan responds with a C1 in 3:4, as he directly contradicts content of God's command. This contradiction of God's word is the only such contradiction recorded in all of Genesis.[9]
- Genesis 3:9 – God calls to Adam, asking where he is. Adam responds with a C1, answering the question in 3:10.
- Genesis 6:13 – God told Noah of His plans to destroy life on earth, and commanded him to make a boat (6:14-16). Noah responded with a C1, building a boat (6:22).

---

[9] While Abram and Sarai responded to God's word with differing degrees of doubt in Genesis 16-18, there was no outright contradiction as there was by Satan in 3:4.

- Genesis 9:1 – God commands Noah and family to multiply, filling the earth.[10] There is no direct response in the immediate context.
- Genesis 9:12 – God discussed the rainbow as the sign of the covenant (9:13). While there is no direct human response in the immediate context, one could interpret the occasional presence of rainbows as a C1 response on the part of nature.
- Genesis 9:17 – God concludes His discussion of the sign of the covenant. No direct response.
- Genesis 15:13 – The proper noun "God" is in the NASB,[11] but not in the BHS.[12] God prophesies a four hundred year enslavement of Abram's descendants. The prophecy is fulfilled literally as a C1, as Israel is enslaved in Egypt for four hundred years, dwelling there for four hundred and thirty (Ex 12:40-41).
- Genesis 17:1 – God introduces Himself to Abram as God Almighty.[13] This address continues through 17:1-16, and has no direct response until 17:17.
- Genesis 17:9 – God continues His address to the newly named Abraham.
- Genesis 17:15 – God continues the monologue, renaming Sarai *Sarah*. Abraham responds in 17:17 with a C1

---

[10] Notably, the dominion mandate is absent from the post-diluvian imperative.
[11] *New American Standard Bible: 1995 Update* (LaHabra, CA: Lockman Foundation, 1995).
[12] Karl Elliger and Wilhelm Rudolph, *Biblia Hebraica Stuttgartensia* (Stuttgart: German Bible Society, 1997).
[13] Heb., *el shaddai*.

evidenced by two actions: (1) laughing in disbelief,[14] and (2) calling his wife by the name God had given her.
- Genesis 17:19 – God reiterates that Sarah would bear a son, that his name should be called Isaac, and that God would keep His covenant through Isaac. God responds with a C1, as He provided a child through Sarah (Gen 21:1-2). Abraham responds with a C1, naming the child Isaac (21:3).
- Genesis 17:23 – This is Abraham's C1 response (with Ishmael and every male of Abraham's household) to God's earlier prescription of circumcision (17:10).
- Genesis 20:3 – God speaks to Abimelech in a dream, addressing him directly without metaphorical language, indicting him for taking the wife of another. Abimelech responds with a C1, asking God a follow-up question.
- Genesis 20:6 – God responds to Abimelech's question with a C1, answering Abimelech's question.
- Genesis 21:12 – God discusses with Abraham the plight of Ishmael and the covenant blessing of Isaac, commanding Abraham to do what Sarah tells him. Abraham responds with a C1, by fulfilling Sarah's request to send Ishmael and Hagar away (21:10, 14).
- Genesis 21:17 – (The angel of) God speaks to comfort Hagar, telling her to lift the boy up and take him by the hand. Hagar's response is to give Ishmael water that God provides, but the text does not indicate how she responded specifically to the command of 21:18.

---

[14] Laughter would be an unnatural response to a preposterous sounding prediction if there was an alternative (to the plain sense of what was verbally expressed) hermeneutic method available.

- Genesis 22:1 – God tells Abraham to slay Isaac. Abraham responds with a C1, to the point of killing Isaac.
- Genesis 26:4 – The Lord appears to Isaac, God speaks to Isaac, introducing Himself as God. Isaac responds with a C1 by worshipping and calling upon the name of the Lord who spoke to him (c.f., 26:24 and 25).
- Genesis 31:11 – Jacob recounts in a C1, how (the angel of) God appears to Jacob in a dream, and how the dream corresponds to what had actually happened earlier (31:7-9).
- Genesis 31:24 – God tells Laban in a dream not to speak to Jacob for "good or bad." Laban responds with a C1, citing God's command as he addresses Jacob carefully so as not to disobey (31:29).
- Genesis 35:1 – God commands Jacob to go to Bethel and make an altar. Jacob responds with a C1, first recounting the command (35:3) and then fulfilling it (35:6-7).
- Genesis 35:10 – God changes Jacob's name to Israel. The writer of Genesis responds with a C1, referring to Jacob as Israel in 35:21-22. The names are used interchangeably from that point forward.
- Genesis 35:11 – God reintroduces Himself to Jacob as God Almighty.[15] Jacob responds with a C1, as he worships the God who spoke to him (35:14-15).
- Genesis 46:2 – God calls out to Jacob in night visions. Jacob responds with a C1, answering the call.
- Genesis 46:3 – God instructs Jacob in a night vision to go to Egypt. Jacob's response is a C1, as he travels to Egypt (46:5-7).

---

[15] Heb., e*l shaddai*, as in 17:1.

While not every "God said" passage includes a direct response in the immediate context, of the twenty-eight direct responses that are immediately recognizable, all but possibly one are obvious C1's, with only Hagar's response in 21:18 not matching exactly the command given her. Hagar's response there doesn't provide evidence for either a C1 or C2. Further, we note from 46:3 that even when God uses dreams to communicate, the intended hermeneutic method is consistent with intended interpretive methodology for things verbally expressed.

The Lord Said (nineteen verses / at least seventeen C1's)
- Genesis 4:6 – The Lord asks Cain why he is angry. Cain responds in 4:8 by telling Abel. Because we are not told *what* Cain told Abel, this is not evidence for a C1 or C2.
- Genesis 4:9 – The Lord asks Cain where is his brother. Cain responds with a C1, answering the question.
- Genesis 4:15 – The Lord put Cain under His own protection. The Lord Himself responds with a C1, appointing a sign for Cain's protection.
- Genesis 6:3 – The Lord limits human lifespan. The set limit is gradually enacted in a C1, as by Moses' lifetime (Deut 34:7), life spans generally begin to fit within that limit.
- Genesis 6:7 – The Lord pronounces that He will destroy man, animals, creeping things, and birds. He reiterates in 6:13, and makes it apparent that He will make some exceptions, by removing some from the path of judgment, including Noah's family, and two of every living species 6:18-20. The Lord responds with a C1 as He brings about the judgment and protects life in 7:1-23.

- Genesis 7:1 – The Lord tells Noah and his family to enter the ark. Noah responds with a C1 as he does all that the Lord had commanded him (7:5).
- Genesis 8:21 – The Lord tells Himself He will never again destroy every living thing as He had done. So far, He has responded with a C1.
- Genesis 11:6 – The Lord acknowledges that a united language provides unique opportunities for human success. The Lord responds with a C1, recognizing the need for and executing the confusing of human language (11:7-8).
- Genesis 12:1 – The Lord told Abram to go. Abram responds with a C1: he went (12:4).
- Genesis 13:14 – The Lord tells Abram He will give to Abram all the land Abram can see. The Lord responds with a C1, reiterating and providing detail for this promise in 15:18-21.
- Genesis 16:9 – The (angel of the) Lord told Hagar to return to Sarai and submit. Hagar responds with a C1, acknowledging that it was the Lord who spoke with her (16:13), and returning to Abram and Sarai (16:15).
- Genesis 16:10 – The (angel of the) Lord promised a multiplying of Ishmael's descendants. The Lord responds with a C1, as evidenced by the early genealogy in 25:12-18.
- Genesis 16:11– The (angel of the) Lord identifies Hagar's pregnancy and prescribes the name Ishmael for the child. Abram responds with a C1, naming the child Ishmael (16:15), which implies a C1 response also on Hagar's part, as it is apparent she relayed the Lord's words to Abram.

- Genesis 18:13 – The Lord questions Sarah regarding her laugh. Sarah responds with a C1, denying the accusation because of fear (18:15).
- Genesis 18:26 – The Lord agrees to spare Sodom if He finds fifty righteous within the city. The Lord responds with a C1, as there weren't fifty (18:32).
- Genesis 22:11 – The (angel of the) Lord calls out to Abraham. Abraham responds with a C1, answering the call.
- Genesis 25:23 – The Lord predicts to Rebekah that there are two nations in her womb, and that the older will serve the younger. Here the Lord employs a metaphor (there were two babies in her womb, not two peoples), but one that would be quite obvious. There is no direct response from Rebekah recorded in the context.
- Genesis 28:13 – The Lord appears to Jacob in a dream, identifying Himself as "the Lord, the God of…Abraham…and Isaac." Jacob responds in worship (28:16-19), an apparent C1.
- Genesis 31:3 – The Lord tells Jacob to return to the land of his fathers. Jacob responds with a C1, returning to Canaan, the land of his father Isaac (31:18).

Again, not every "the Lord said" passage includes a direct response in the immediate context. Still, of the seventeen direct responses that are immediately obvious, they are all C1's. In Genesis 25:23 there is a notable metaphor employed (two nations in Rebekah's womb), with no direct response from Rebekah. While it would seem that the meaning of the metaphor would be entirely obvious to any listener, it is worth noting that the prediction came to pass in a literal way at least during

David's rule (2 Sam 8:14). This instance illustrates that when metaphorical language is used in the text it is used in such a way as to be readily discernible as metaphor, and figurative usage does not alter the intended hermeneutic method or the outcome.

The Lord God Said (five verses / at least four C1's)
- Genesis 2:16 – The Lord God prohibits the man from eating of the tree of the knowledge of good and evil (2:17). Eve responds in 3:2-3 with a C1, though she adds a condition (touching also prohibited). Adam responds in 3:12 with a C1, acknowledging that God was speaking of a literal tree, from which Adam had eaten.
- Genesis 2:18 – The Lord God announced He would make a helper for Adam. The Lord God responded with a C1, creating Eve (2:22).
- Genesis 3:13 – The Lord God asks Eve what she had done. Eve responds with a C1, answering the question according to the events that occurred.
- Genesis 3:14 – The Lord God pronounces judgment on the serpent: it is cursed, will travel on its belly and eat dust; and in 3:15, there will be enmity with woman and her seed (singular), it will crush seed on the heel and be crushed on the head. Each of these judgments appears to be literally fulfilled as C1's, though the seed references are singular and may reference an individual (Messiah?) rather than simply men in general. In providing the only direct response to the entire judgment passage, Eve seems to respond with a C1, as she seemingly anticipates literal fulfillment in the form of a specific individual when she rejoices that a seed seems to be provided (Gen 4:1).

- Genesis 3:22 – The Lord God observes the potential danger of man eating from the tree of life and living forever in a cursed state. The Lord God responds with a C1, as He drives man out of the garden, and prohibits his return (3:23-24).

"The Lord God said" references are all found in the second and third chapters of Genesis. Though 3:14-15 presents some special challenges, the statements made there seem to be best understood as C1's. At the very least we can say there is no evidence in that passage supporting a C2 understanding by any of the original listeners. Each of the other four references provides obvious C1 responses.

He Said (twenty-four verses /at least twenty-three C1's)
- Genesis 3:11 – He asks Adam[16] if he had eaten from the tree. Adam responds with a C1, answering in the affirmative (3:12).
- Genesis 3:16 – He pronounces judgment on the woman: multiplied pain in childbirth, "upon your man shall be your longing," and" it shall be that he shall rule in you." The pains of labor would seem to support a C1 understanding. The woman would desire her man. The exact meaning of "he shall rule in you" is not clear. To clarify, the NASB translates the preposition as "over" rather than "in" – implying either a sexual connotation or a non-egalitarian position (not prescribed here, just described, if that is the meaning), but that seems not to be an accurate translation. In any case, there is no

---
[16] As indicated by the second person singular masculine pronominal suffix.

evidence to suggest anything other than a C1 meaning here.

- Genesis 3:17 – Adam – ground cursed, providing food but with difficulty for Adam, Adam will return to the ground (in death). Experience demonstrates the difficulty of growing food. Further, Adam physically died (5:5), supporting the idea that these judgments also are intended as C1's.
- Genesis 4:10 – He asks Cain what he had done, and pronounced judgment (4:11-12). Cain responds with a C1, lamenting that the punishment was too severe (4:13).
- Genesis 15:5 – He pronounces that Abraham's descendants would be more numerous than the stars Abraham could count. Abraham responds famously with a C1 by believing in the Lord and being credited with righteousness (15:6).
- Genesis 15:7 – He identifies Himself to Abraham as the Lord who brought Abraham out of Ur. The statement is a C1 interpretation of 12:1-4, which described Abraham's departure from Ur.
- Genesis 15:9 – He told Abraham to bring Him specific animals. Abraham responds with a C1, as Abraham brings those specific things to God (15:10).
- Genesis 16:8 – He asks Hagar from whence she came. Hagar responds with a C1, answering the question directly.
- Genesis 18:10 – He announced that the following year Sarah would have a son. Sarah responds with a C1, interpreting the prediction literally and laughing at the possibility (18:12). God responds with a C1, as He provided for Sarah a son at the appointed time (21:1-2).

- Genesis 18:15 – He reiterated that Sarah did laugh. His comment was a C1 interpretation of 18:12, for she indeed did laugh.
- Genesis 18:28 – He said He would not destroy the city if there were forty-five. His response was a C1, as He apparently knew that the number was less than ten (18:32).
- Genesis 18:29 – He said He would not destroy the city if there were forty. His response was a C1, as He apparently knew that the number was less than ten (18:32).
- Genesis 18:30 – He said He would not destroy the city if there were thirty. His response was a C1, as He apparently knew that the number was less than ten (18:32).
- Genesis 18:31 – He said He would not destroy the city if there were twenty. His response was a C1, as He apparently knew that the number was less than ten (18:32).
- Genesis 18:32 – He said He would not destroy the city if there were ten. His response was a C1, as He destroyed the city, because there were not ten righteous in the city (19:13, 24-25).
- Genesis 22:2 – He tells Abraham to take Isaac to Moriah and to offer him as a sacrifice on a mountain He would specify. Abraham responds with C1's to all three commands (22:3, 9), stopping only at the point the angel of the Lord calls out to him (22:11).
- Genesis 22:12 – He tells Abraham not to Isaac. Abraham responds with a C1, locating and alternative offering of God's provision (22:13-14).

- Genesis 31:12 – He directs Jacob to consider how He has provided for Jacob, as a C1 interpretation of 31:10.
- Genesis 32:26 – He asks Jacob to let Him go. Jacob responds with a C1, refusing to let Him go unless He first gives Jacob a blessing.
- Genesis 32:27 – He asks Jacob what is his name. Jacob responds with a C1, replying with his name.
- Genesis 32:28 – He changes Jacob's name to Israel. The writer of Genesis responds with a C1, acknowledging the name Israel for Jacob in 35:21-22.
- Genesis 32:29 – As a C1 response to Jacob's question, He questions in return why Jacob wants to know His name.
- Genesis 46:3 – He encourages Jacob not to be afraid to go to Egypt. Jacob responds with a C1, as he goes to Egypt (46:6).
- Genesis 48:4 – Jacob recounts God Almighty's appearing to him at Luz, and His promise of blessing to his descendants. Jacob responds with a C1, as he claims two of Joseph's sons as his own, so that they will be blessed under the promise God had given him (48:5).

In all twenty-four instances of "He said" that are directly attributable to God, we discover C1 responses that are readily identifiable. Only 3:16 offers any challenge at all, and even that passage, describing Eve's judgment can be viewed as understood by her with a C1 approach, particularly in light of her response in 4:1. It can at least be said here as well that there is no evidence of any C2 responses. Thus the "He said" passages constitute at least twenty-three additional clear C1 responses.

The Speech Acts of God and Responses in Job Confirm the Literal Grammatical Historical Hermeneutic of Genesis

Other than the eighty-four verses in Genesis evidencing a model for interpreting Scripture, there are ten similar passages in Job that provide a secondary support to the monolithic hermeneutic method evident thus far in Genesis. In each instance of Divine speech acts in Job, the speaker is identified as "the Lord."[17]

The Lord Said (ten verses / ten C1's)
- Job 1:7 – The Lord asks Satan from whence he came. Satan responds with a C1 ("From roaming about on the earth and walking around on it.").
- Job 1:8 – The Lord asks Satan if he has considered Job. Satan responds in 1:9 with a C1 (an implied yes, and a suggestion of why Job was righteous).
- Job 1:12 – The Lord commissions Satan to do all but harm Job physically. Satan responds in 1:12-19 with a C1, both in departing to fulfill the commission, and also in only harming Job's belongings.
- Job 2:2 – The Lord asks Satan again from whence he came. Satan responds with the same C1 response as in 1:7.
- Job 2:3 – The Lord asks Satan again if he has considered Job. Satan responds in 2:4 with a C1, adding that Job was only righteous because of his health.
- Job 2:6 – The Lord gives permission for Satan to harm Job, but not to the extent of taking his life. Satan

---

[17] Heb. *Yahweh*.

responds in 2:7 with a C1, smiting Job with boils, but not taking his life.
- Job 38:1 – The Lord answered Job in chapters 38-39 using a serious of graphic illustrations of God's sovereignty over nature. There is no response from Job, at this point.
- Job 40:1 – The Lord challenges Job to respond. Job responds in 40:3-5 with a C1, recognizing his own insignificance in comparison to the Lord.
- Job 40:6 – The Lord answers Job again, in chapters 40-41 reiterating His sovereignty over nature, using some metaphorical language to describe creatures He designed. Job responds by repenting in 42:1-6 with a C1, indicating that he recognized the purpose of the metaphorical language as supportive of God's thesis that He governs nature.
- Job 42:7 – The Lord communicates his anger toward Job's three friends, and commands them to take an offering to Job. The three respond in 42:9 with a C1, doing exactly "as the Lord told them." Further, God demonstrated a C1 response by accepting their actions in 42:9.

In these ten verses, we find ten C1's and zero C2's. Notably, one of the C1 responses is from God, Himself. Job's record of God's speech acts and the responses indicates there is no deviation from the pattern modeled in Genesis. Further, Job's response to God's use of metaphorical language in chapters 40-41 indicates that the Divine use of figurative language did not change the expectation that what was verbally expressed should be interpreted in a basic, face-value, common-sense way. In short, the addition of figurative language did not result in any adjustment to the hermeneutic method.

Conclusion

In examination of the ninety-four passages in Genesis and Job that record Divine speech acts, the evidence is overwhelming (*eighty-one C1's to absolutely zero C2's*) that God intended for His words to be taken at face value, using a plain-sense interpretive approach. The hermeneutic method that reflects this straightforward methodology has become known as the *literal grammatical historical hermeneutic*. This method recognizes that verbal expression has meaning rooted in and inseparable from the grammatical and historical context of the language used, and that these components require that readers be consistent in applying the interpretive method in their study of the Scriptures.

Because of the two-thousand-year precedent evident in Genesis and Job, any departure from the simplicity of this method bears a strong exegetical burden of proof, requiring that there be *explicit exegetical support for any change one might perceive as necessary in handling later Scriptures*. Absent any such exegetical data, we can conclude that (1) hermeneutic methodology for understanding Scripture is not arbitrary but is instead plainly modeled, and that (2) later Scriptures should be understood in light of the hermeneutic precedent provided by Genesis and Job.

5
PRIORITY OF EPISTEMOLOGICAL FOUNDATIONS IN THEOLOGICAL METHOD:
BOB'S CRAZY DAY WITH THE DANDELIONS[18]

Of the four major components of philosophy and worldview (epistemology, metaphysics, ethics, and socio-political thought), none can be adequately addressed until we answer the question of *how* we can know. Regarding metaphysics, for example, we can't make legitimate assertions about the character of God or the existence of the human soul until we first address how such assertions can be verified or falsified. Further, unless we have a means for validating ethical prescriptions as either worthy or unworthy, we have no warrant for choosing one prescription over another – especially when we encounter apparently competing or conflicting goods. And if we have no mechanism for authentication, then how can we even arrive at a definition of *what is good* in the first place? Finally, in socio-political thought, on what basis can we choose one system of government over another, or how can we determine whether a law is commendable? Without correct epistemological answers, there is no basis for our understanding or choosing one

---

[18] Originally presented to the Chafer Theological Seminary Conference, Houston, Texas, March 20, 2014.

thing over another. In short, epistemology is really about authority, verifiability, truth, and certainty.

Imagine a person – we'll call him Bob. Bob has just received the gift of consciousness. For the first time in Bob's existence he is *aware*. Bob examines his surroundings and he finds himself standing in rolling sun-drenched fields of dandelions under a beautifully clear mid-day sky. Of course, Bob has no knowledge of what anything around him is or what any of it means, because this is the first time he has ever encountered any of these things. Bob begins to ponder. *"Here I am, I suppose, now what?"* Bob has to figure out how to answer that question before he takes his first step, lest he make the wrong assumptions and step in the wrong direction. He begins a quest to decipher the right understanding of who and what he is, and how he must proceed, but he isn't certain of whether or not he has the right tools for the task. In fact, he isn't certain of anything.

Descartes' Rationalism

Rene Descartes engaged a similar exercise in his *Meditations*. He first describes things that we may doubt, acknowledging that the senses sometimes deceive us, and that "it is the part of prudence not to place absolute confidence in that by which we have even once been deceived."[19] Descartes begins with the assumption that a benevolent God exists who allows people sometimes to fooled by their senses, and Descartes considers that if God allows for occasional deceptions, it is theoretically possible that God, Himself, is constantly deceptive (though Descartes ultimately concludes that God is not

---

[19] Rene Descartes, *Meditations*, trans. John Veitch, 1901, 1:3.

deceptive). Descartes wonders how we can come to certainty of truth if instead of a benevolent God there exists a malevolent demon that is constantly deceiving us. Descartes engages a process of elimination to discover the things that cannot be doubted, irrespective of the existence and nature of God. He concludes, "I am, I exist, is necessarily true each time it is expressed by me, or conceived in my mind."[20] Descartes suggests that his own thinking is verification of his existence, and cannot be doubted. This is the *cogito ergo sum* (I think therefore I am)[21] which undergirds his epistemology. Because Descartes considers reason as something that cannot be doubted, he values it above all else. With respect to the existence of God, for example, Descartes reasons *to* the existence of God, and the existence and nature of God is ultimately subject to the guided use of reason. In the end, Descartes' epistemology undermines any authority claimed by special revelation, instead depending on reason guided by method as the ultimate arbiter of truth.

Hume's Naturalistic Empiricism

Unlike Descartes, David Hume values experience over reason. Hume distinguishes between thoughts or ideas and impressions or perceptions, preferring the latter as more reliable for discovering truth. He explains:

> All ideas, especially abstract ones, are naturally faint and obscure: the mind has but a slender hold on them; they are apt to be confounded with other resembling ideas...on the contrary, all impressions, that is, all sensations,

---

[20] *Meditations*, 2:3.
[21] Found in Descartes', *Discourse on the Method of Rightly Conducting the Reason, and Seeking Truth in the Sciences*, Part IV.

either outward or inward, are strong and vivid; the limits between them are more exactly determined; nor is it easy to fall into any error or mistake with regard to them.[22]

Hume adds that this proposition, understood properly, "might render every dispute equally intelligible, and banish all that jargon, which has so long taken possession of metaphysical reasonings, and drawn disgrace upon them."[23] Hume suggests that in order to resolve metaphysical questions we must prioritize impressions over ideas. This leads Hume to conclude against the metaphysical, because he argues that there are no true impressions of the supernatural. For example, with respect to miracles, Hume asserts that,

> no testimony is sufficient to establish a miracle, unless the testimony be of such a kind that its falsehood would be more miraculous…When anyone tells me that he saw a dead man restored to life, I immediately consider with myself whether it be more probable that this person should either deceive or be deceived, or that the fact which he relates should really have happened…[24]

Hume is pre-committed to the least miraculous outcome – that which is least likely to violate experiential norms. This illustrates his understandable but inadequately justified dependence on the senses for ascertaining reality. Hume's

---

[22] Excerpt from David Hume's *An Enquiry Concerning Human Understanding*, as quoted in Christopher Cone, *Life Beyond the Sun: An Introduction to Worldview and Philosophy Through the Lens of Ecclesiastes* (Fort Worth, TX: Tyndale Seminary Press, 2009), 32-33.
[23] Ibid., 32.
[24] Ibid., 34.

epistemology can be correct insofar as his impressions and their interpretations are accurate, but wherever the senses are limited in scope there is much potential for error.

Nietzsche's Existentialism

Friedrich Nietzsche seems driven by a pre-commitment to skepticism of absolute moral value. While he does not fully develop a theory of the mind,[25] he does affirm some definitive epistemological principles. Phenomenal reality (or experiences) can be verified by the senses, but noumenal (or absolute) reality cannot be verified at all. Nietzsche does not necessarily deny that absolute meaning exists, but he argues we can't interface directly with it if it does exist; consequently, absolute reality and meaning are irrelevant to us, therefore we must make our own realities.

Nietzsche's agnostic assertion that *we cannot know* leads him to a curiously confident metaphysical interpretation and ethical prescription:

> I entreat you, my brothers, remain true to the earth, and do not believe those who speak to you of superterrestrial hopes! They are poisoners, whether they know it or not. They are despisers of life, atrophying and self-poisoned men, of whom the earth is weary: so let them begone![26]

---

[25] Brian Leiter, *Routledge Philosophy Guidebook to Nietzsche on Morality* (New York: Routledge, 2002), 87.
[26] Excerpt from Nietzsche's *Thus Spake Zarathustra*, as quoted in Christopher Cone, *Life Beyond the Sun: An Introduction to Worldview and Philosophy Through the Lens of Ecclesiastes* (Fort Worth, TX: Tyndale Seminary Press, 2009), 323.

As Nietzsche generally asserts that we cannot know, he does seem certain in his knowledge that we cannot know. In this inconsistency it is illustrated that his epistemology is less an attempt to coherently interpret knowledge than it is a mechanism to justify his amoral pre-commitment. In this Nietzsche shows that his first step is an assertion of will rather than an objective attempt to understand reality. In fact, Nietzsche's ultimate prescription for humanity is the culmination of that assertion of will:

> That is your entire will, you wisest men; it is a will to power; and that is so even when you talk of good and evil and of the assessment of values...Where I found a living creature, there I found will to power; and even in the will of the servant I found the will to be master.[27]

In Nietzsche's thinking, especially, we see the intersection of the four major components of philosophy and worldview (epistemology, metaphysics, ethics, and socio-political thought), and the impossibility of practical agnosticism applied in these areas. These components demand commitment, and Nietzsche exposes inconsistency in the assumptions and conclusions of the agnostic commitment.

The views of Descartes, Hume, and Nietzsche represent three prominent epistemological perspectives undergirding worldview. For Descartes, reason is the ultimate arbiter of truth, and we can know with certainty by the proper use of reason. For Hume, experience is the ultimate arbiter of truth, and we can know with certainty through sensory verification. For Nietzsche,

---

[27] Ibid., 326.

we cannot know with certainty, therefore we must simply pursue what is valuable to us.

The Bible offers an alternative epistemological model. Remember Bob? Imagine Bob standing in the field taking in and considering the new sights, sounds, smells, and sensations he is experiencing. He looks down and sees a Bible at his feet. He bends down, and reaching out his hands he picks up the Bible. He opens it, and recognizing that the words on the pages are orderly and expressive representations of meaning – just like his own thoughts are – he begins to read in Genesis. He continues through the entire Bible, and then closes it, gazing around him one last time before taking his first step. His first thought after gaining consciousness was, *"here I am, I suppose, now what?"* The Bible answers the question for him, and encourages him to take his first step. But how?

A Biblical Epistemology

The first epistemological statement in the Bible is actually made by the serpent in the Garden: "For God knows that in the day you eat from it your eyes will be opened, and you will be like God, knowing good and evil" (Gen 3:5). Satan prescribes knowledge through contradicting God's design for knowledge. The fact that Satan chose epistemology as an early battleground underscores the strategic significance of epistemology in God's design. In this context Satan challenges Eve to consider a different starting point than God had prescribed, and if she does, Satan promises, Eve will have a better outcome – that her knowledge will be more complete, even to the point of making her godlike. While the actions Satan prescribed *did* result in particular knowledge (Gen 3:22), it was a distortion of God's design for knowledge and resulted in tragedy and not blessing. These events invite the reader to inquire as to God's ideal for human knowledge, and the answer is provided especially in the writings of Solomon, to whom it was granted to be exceedingly wise (1 Kin 3:12).

In the book of Proverbs Solomon identifies the first epistemological step undergirding a Biblical worldview: "The fear of the Lord is the beginning of wisdom" (Prov 1:7); "The fear of the Lord is the beginning of wisdom, and the knowledge of the Holy One is understanding" (Prov 9:10); and again, "The fear of the Lord is the instruction for wisdom" (Prov 15:33). The word for wisdom is the Hebrew *yirah*, and does not simply denote respect, but is the term normally used of fear – as in fear for one's life.[28] In context, the fear of the Lord involves the right perspective of and response to God.[29] Though Solomon uses a different word for fear in Proverbs 28:14, the contrast to appropriate fear is hardness of heart.[30] In short, the fear of the Lord involves the inner man's responsiveness to God. Notice the critique of the atheist in Psalm 14:1: "The fool has said in his *heart* (Heb., *leb*) 'There is no God.'" The fool is unresponsive toward God, and sets his will against God, whereas the one who would possess wisdom acknowledges God and is responsive to Him.

From whence comes the fear of the Lord? "For the Lord gives wisdom; from His mouth comes wisdom and understanding" (Prov 2:6). If the first step or first principle of Biblical epistemology is to fear the Lord, the authoritative

---

[28] E.g., Gen 15:1, 32:11; Prov 3:25, etc.
[29] Discussions regarding the fear the Lord are found also in the NT in passages such as Romans 3:18; 2 Corinthians 5:11, 7:1; Ephesians 5:21; 1 Peter 2:17; and Revelation 14:7.
[30] The Hebrew *leb*, translated here as *heart*, is generally used to reference the heart, mind, will, and/or inner man.

source for the data we need to do so is identified as Scripture itself – a revelation which presupposes the existence of the Biblical God, and makes no effort to defend that first and most vital principle. So when Bob begins to read the Bible, he discovers therein the limitations of human reasoning – and thus, the inadequacies of rationalism (Gen 6:5; 1 Cor 2:14); he encounters the limited scope of human experience and of the uninformed arrogance of naturalistic empiricism (Job 38:4, 34-35, 39:26-27, 41:11, 42:5-6); and he discovers that there is indeed discernable meaning and truth – *noumenal reality*, created and revealed by God, and relevant for everyday human life – even if God hasn't revealed its fullness (Ecc 3:11; Jn 20:31; Jam 3:17-18; 1 Jn 5:13).

Bob is left with an important choice, and he must choose between mutually exclusive first principles: rationalism, naturalistic empiricism, existentialism, or Biblical presuppositionalism.[31] Each of the four claims to be the arbiter of truth, and each demands presuppositions regarding the nature of evidence. Rationalism requires total trust in human reason, naturalistic empiricism is premised on the complete reliability of the senses, existentialism demands practical certainty in the idea that there can be no certainty, and Biblical presuppositionalism bids us trust in the words of a book that Bob found in a field of dandelions – a book that claims to be God's

---

[31] The term *presuppositionalism* is borrowed from Cornelius Van Til, and is employed here to account for the idea that the Bible presupposes, rather than defends, the existence of God, and that according to the Bible the proper understanding of reality depends entirely on and works from the acceptance of that presupposition – *that the God of the Bible exists*. In other words, whereas rationalism argues *to* God, and naturalistic empiricism and existentialism argue *against* God, Biblical presuppositionalism argues *from* God.

word, and the only way to have certainty regarding who and what we actually are. Whichever of these options Bob selects will – if he is consistent in its application – set the course of his entire worldview, whether he realizes it or not. C'mon, Bob. We're counting on you. Do the right thing. But Bob has a problem, and, having read the book, he is beginning to understand that problem.

Four Pillars

Some years ago I published a paper, entitled "Presuppositional Dispensationalism,"[32] in which I attempted to summarize the Biblical epistemological model with the illustration of four pillars. Pillar #1 is the existence of the Biblical God. As first principal, the God of the Bible exists, and not merely as one god among many, but as the One who has disclosed Himself in such a way that His exclusivity is unavoidable. Further, He is characterized above all else by *holiness* (Is 6:3; Rev 4:8), and all that He does is to be understood through that lens. The recognition of this first principle does not advocate *faith* as the sole or final source of understanding

---

[32] Originally published as Christopher Cone, "Presuppositional Dispensationalism" in *The Conservative Theological Journal*, Volume 10, Issue 29 (May 2006), presently accessible with permission at http://www.drcone.com/2012/09/23/presuppositional-dispensationalism-part-1/, and later expanded into a dissertation entitled, "Prolegomena: A Survey and Introduction to Method in Theology, Beginning With Presuppositional Epistemology and Resulting in Normative Dispensationalism," and is presently available in its revised and expanded form as *Prolegomena on Biblical Hermeneutics and Method* (TSP, 2012).

truth;[33] rather it is an invitation to step into the Biblical perspective, to "taste and see that the Lord is good" (Ps 34:8).

Pillar #2 is the principle that God has divinely and authoritatively disclosed Himself for the purpose of His own glorification, through general revelation (creation, Rom 1:18-20), special revelation (the Bible, 2 Tim 3:16-17), and personal revelation (Jesus Christ, Jn 1:1-18). General revelation renders every man without excuse, providing an inescapable awareness of God. But general revelation is intentionally incomplete and ineffective for providing regenerative grace – special and personal revelation is needed for that. In special revelation God chose human language as the vehicle for His self-disclosure. As evidenced by His use of it, language is a reliable medium for God's communication. Consequently, insofar as God has revealed Himself in Scripture, He may be understood. As the product of the self-disclosing God who speaks with authority as the Creator, the Bible does not appeal to human reason nor to human experience as proof of its authenticity. Rather the Bible presents itself to humanity as possessing the requisite authority, and renders humanity accountable for our response to that authority. A central theme of the Bible is its description of God's personal revelation through Jesus Christ. He is the way, the truth, and the life, and provides for us the payment for and offer of life. *"Taste and see that the Lord is good" (Ps 34:8).*

Pillar #3 is the incapacity of natural man to comprehend (receive) God's revelation. Of course, humanity can cognitively understand and experientially interact with general and special revelation, and is enlightened further in Christ's incarnation (Jn 1:9), but just as natural man rejects that which we know about

---

[33] Thus Biblical presuppositionalism is not subject to the charge of fideism.

God through creation (Rom 1:18-20), and just as natural man fails to receive the spiritual truths of the word (1 Cor 2:14), natural man likewise rejects God's revelation in the Person of Christ (Jn 3:19). This is not just Bob's problem, it is yours and mine as well: without some type of additional divine aid, humanity consistently fails to receive that which God has revealed. Humanity is characterized by sin, depravity, and brokenness (or deadness) in the apparatus for thinking, feeling, and choosing. Importantly, this is why simple mental ascent to Biblical principles is not sufficient for accomplishing the fundamental change necessary. We don't move from death unto life simply by means of thinking rightly. It is here that we see the limitations of epistemology: a correct understanding of the Biblical design does not save, even though it allows us to interact with and understand accurately the data we need. But God[34] the Father draws (Jn 6:44), chooses (Rom 9:15-16; Eph 1:4-6), and calls (Gal 1:4-6); God the Son reveals (Jn 1:9) and redeems (Eph 1:7); and God the Spirit convicts (Jn 16:8) and enables (1 Cor 12:3). There is divine enablement needed and provided, according to His own will, for overcoming the deficiencies of humanity inherited through sin.

Pillar #4 is the necessity of a consistently applied hermeneutic. Scripture claims God-breathed authority and has been revealed in particular known human languages that are composed of finite vocabularies and grammatical concepts. These two principles demand two corresponding hermeneutic principles: (1) that we understand the meaning of the text in the normal sense of these languages (i.e., the literal grammatical

---

[34] Notice that in the two key Biblical discussions of how we move from death unto life, the transition is introduced by the words, "But...God" (Rom 3:21 ; Eph 2:4).

historical hermeneutic), and (2) that we are hermeneutically consistent in deference to the authority of the text, and in recognition that it is the Revealer who is enthroned and not the interpreter.

The conclusions derived through application of this natural way of handling the text are decisively premillennial and dispensational. Even opponents of dispensational conclusions admit that those conclusions are grounded in a literal approach. As outspoken non-dispensationalist John Gerstner asserts, "on points where we differ there is a tendency for dispensationalists to be literalistic where the non-dispensationalist tends to interpret the Bible figuratively."[35] Because the Biblical epistemological model demands a consistent literal grammatical historical hermeneutic, and dispensationalism is grounded in that hermeneutic more than any other theological system, in comparison to other theological systems, dispensational theology best follows the Biblical epistemological model. But *best* isn't good enough if dispensationalism is simply the least inaccurate of many inaccurate systems. We should not strive simply to be better than other deficient systems, rather we should strive to be Biblically accurate in *every* aspect. Our pursuit is *a more Biblical theology*, and that pursuit demands careful adherence to Biblical epistemology. Bob doesn't need a better explanation; he needs *the truth*!

Implications for Theology

Sadly, in the past few hundred years of more formalized dispensational thought, it seems dispensationalists, in

---

[35] John Gerstner, *Wrongly Dividing the Word of Truth* (Morgan, PA: Sole Deo Gloria, 2000), 93.

comparison to other theological traditions, have devoted little effort to epistemology. If one were to Google the phrase *dispensational epistemology*, they might be shocked (perhaps even appalled) at the novelty of the most popular results. That simple exercise is indicative of our historical deficiency in this area. Instead of doing our own work, and discovering a Biblical theology from the ground up, working from sound (i.e., Biblical) first principles, we have borrowed extensively from theoreticians in the Thomistic and Reformed traditions. Thomism is quite at home with rationalism, predating Descartes' version. Reformed epistemology is not far removed from the Biblical model, but Reformed theological pre-commitments (like replacement theology) are justified through methodological inconsistencies. As grand as are the successes of Cornelius Van Til's presuppositional thought, for example, his theologically driven hermeneutical inconsistencies are equally magnificent in their failings.[36]

---

[36] One example of such inconsistency is in Van Til's equating of Israel and the church, a characteristic *one people of God* doctrine within Reformed theology, and one that Van Til assumes, rather than defends: "...The Israel of God was tired of building alone, and was gradually accepting of more aid from the Samaritans. The antithesis between the church and the world was dying out..." (from Cornelius Van Til, *A Survey of Christian Epistemology* (Philllipsburg, NJ: P&R Publishing, 1969), 61.); "Here, in the midst of this people Israel and nowhere else, the true obedience, the true patience, and the true hope of faith was found. As in the ark the family, the church, and human culture were preserved and redeemed..." (from Cornelius Van Til, *Essays on Christian Education* (Philllipsburg, NJ: P&R Publishing, 1979), 25.); "Christianity is here as elsewhere restorative. And this is true of the Old Testament dispensation as well as of the New..." (from Cornelius Van Til, "The Ten Commandments" (65-page syllabus from Westminster Theological Seminary, 1933), 58.).

Rather than depending upon inconsistently applied methodology for the discovery of our theology, it would be far better to ascertain a Biblical methodology, to apply it consistently, and to allow the theological chips to fall where they may. In short, our loyalty must not be to a theological tradition – dispensational or otherwise. Instead, our loyalty lies where He tells us we find wisdom: *in His word*. Now, of course, we recognize that the Bible understood through the lens of the literal grammatical historical hermeneutic produces dispensational conclusions. Of course we recognize that the primary hallmark of dispensational theology is its usually effective commitment to being Biblically derived, but we cannot with one hand claim to be Biblical in our methodology when with the other hand we are methodologically inconsistent (unless we are willing to assert that the Bible itself prescribes an inconsistent method, and I, for the record, am not).

Dispensationalism is absolutely not a hermeneutic. It should be, on the other hand, simply the product of a methodology and a hermeneutic *consistently applied*. If we treat dispensational theology itself as a hermeneutic lens, then we are no better off than those who appeal to historical theology as their authority for understanding Scripture (as the Catholic Catechism prescribes its followers must do[37]). Consequently, the prescription for a more Biblical theology is not that we do *more theology*, it is that we be *more Biblical* – and that starts with a Biblical epistemology, which reveals a Biblical hermeneutic (literal grammatical historical), and results in Biblical conclusions.

---

[37] see *Catechism of the Catholic Church* (New York: Doubleday, 1995), Prologue III:11; Part 1, Article 2:III:92; and especially Part 1, Article 3:III:113.

Conclusion

Just as Bob stood amidst the dandelions looking for answers, we all face (consciously or not) the same epistemological questions as we take our first steps in the pursuit of truth. Unfortunately, often we don't test the answers ourselves, deferring instead to the efforts of *thinkers* like Descartes, *feelers* like Hume, and *willers* like Nietzsche. In so doing, we fail to properly evaluate how first principles set the course of our entire worldview. This failure contributes to our own misunderstanding of reality – both in theory and practice, and it detracts from our ability to account for the sometimes-gigantic differences between us in how we understand that reality. Our epistemological differences are at the very core of our metaphysical and ethical differences. Whether we realize it or not, our disagreements are not grounded as much in conclusions as they are in our epistemological methodology.

If we are employing non-Biblical methodology for explaining reality, then our conclusions will generally be incongruent with the Biblical data. If this is so, then why have we given so little attention to these foundational issues? It is one thing to say that the Bible is our authority; it is another to *actually do theology, philosophy and worldview – to do life* – that way. When any aspect of our theology is grounded on any authority other than the Bible itself, it is highly unlikely, if not impossible, that we will arrive at purely Biblical conclusions. When we borrow from other worldviews to ground our theology, then we should not be surprised at the systematic inconsistencies that arise. On the other hand, if we answer the epistemological questions correctly, then we can base our subsequent steps on the proper authority. As a result, we are able, by His design and through His assistance, to confidently *verify* truth. This makes Bob very happy.

6
PRIORITY OF AUTHENTICITY IN THE SOURCE OF AUTHORITY

John Locke deftly identifies the central problem of Biblical authority: he explains that if all of holy writ is to be equally considered as inspired of God, then there is much to be questioned regarding the Christian faith;[38] however, if it is not to be so considered, then the authority of the text may be questioned and ultimately undermined, and thus the Christian faith comes crumbling down.[39] Quite a problem indeed. If the text is not authoritative then hermeneutic exercises are quite inconsequential for any purposes other than literary appreciation. Thus the authority of the text is central at this point. How then does Biblical criticism influence the discussion? And what can be said of authority after the text has been submitted to the critical processes?

Louis Wallis keenly summarizes the rise of Biblical criticism, observing correctly that it did not originate in the minds of German scholars, but instead enjoyed a more eclectic genesis. His comments trace progress from the twelfth to the eighteenth century, and their thoroughness and conciseness

---

[38] E.S. de Beer, ed., The Correspondence of John Locke, Vol. 2 (Oxford: Clarendon Press, 1979), 2:748-751 (No. 834).

[39] John Marshall, John Locke: Resistance, Religion and Responsibility, (Cambridge, MA: Cambridge University Press, 1994), 340.

warrant their full representation here. He describes the rise of Biblical criticism as follows:

> ...distinctly foreshadowed by a Spanish Jew, Ibn Ezra, the most eminent Biblical scholar of the Middle Ages, far back in the twelfth century A.D. The idea was taken up by the English scholar Hobbes, in his book, Leviathan, published in 1651; by the Frenchman L Peyrere, in his book Pre-Adamites, issued in 1655; and by the Jewish philosopher Spinoza, of Amsterdam, Holland, in Tractatus-Theologico-Politicus, which came out in 1670. In the meanwhile the Frenchman Louis Cappellus in 1650 published his Critica Sacra, demonstrating the imperfect and fallible condition of the Hebrew vowel points. In 1678, Richard Simon, another Frenchman, put forth a volume entitled Critical History of the Old Testament, showing that the Mosaic Law was compiled and edited centuries after the time of Moses. In 1753 appeared a work by Astruc, a French writer, identifying the so-called Jehovist and Elohist documents in Genesis. In 1800 was published the Critical Remarks of Alexander Geddes, a Scotchman, who denied the Mosaic authorship of the Pentateuch. And although German scholars in the nineteenth century did more for Biblical interpretation than did the scholars of other countries, they were matched in critical acumen during that period by Renan of France, Colenso of England, and Kuenen of Holland.[40]

---

[40] Louis Wallis, "The Paradox of Modern Biblical Criticism" in The Biblical World, Vol. 52, No. 1 (Jul. 1918): 42-43.

Notably, two of the earlier critics cited by Wallis, Ibn Ezra and Spinoza, built on earlier traditions. Fred G. Bratton suggests they borrowed from the Talmudists, "who called attention to scores of discrepancies and contradictions in the Old Testament."[41] Bratton provides a series of examples, citing observations "by one that the flood was not a world catastrophe but local in character, by another that Moses and Elijah did not ascend to heaven, and by a third that the birds which fed Elijah were human."[42]

In the ninth century, Hivi[43] considered Bible difficulties, resolving some of them in anticipation of "rationalistic exegesis."[44] Another scholar, whose name is unknown but whose eleventh century work does Schecter describe, draws attention to every perceived Old Testament discrepancy.[45] The earlier Talmudists, and these two later textual critics along with Origen and his hermeneutic apologetics show that Biblical criticism is not simply a modern affair. Nonetheless, modernity gave rise to such a degree of refinement in Biblical criticism that that the inspiration of the text – and consequently its authority as a moral undergirding – has been widely doubted.

The twelfth-century Abraham Ibn Ezra, questioned Mosaic authorship of the Pentateuch based on retrospective language that seemed to look back from a vantage point well beyond the years of Moses' lifetime. Additionally, Ezra was the first to assert plural authorship of Isaiah, citing, for example, that references to Cyrus as Israel's deliverer could not have been

---

[41] Fred G. Bratton, "Precursors of Biblical Criticism" in Journal of Biblical Literature, Vol. 50, No. 3 (1931): 180.
[42] Fred G. Bratton, "Precursors of Biblical Criticism", 180.
[43] Talmudist cited by Bratton: 180.
[44] Bratton: 180.
[45] Ibid.

penned by the eighth-century Isaiah.[46] Despite his questioning of the text in these specific regards, he had great respect for it, considering it worthy of study. His precise understanding of the Hebrew language allowed him to offer clarifications where others had difficulty; this lent him such a high degree of credibility that he is perceived as a bridge from ancient to modern Biblical scholarship.[47]

Hobbes takes up the discussion in 1651 in the thirty-third chapter of his Leviathan,[48] in which he questions the authorship of Moses. He discusses a few specific cases which seem to cast doubt on Moses' authorship of the Torah. He cites Deuteronomy 34, which includes the account of Moses' death – how he journeys up a mountain views the promised land which he was forbidden from entering due to a moment of rebellion, how he dies, and how God dispensed with Moses' body and it was never discovered. Hobbes asserts that Moses could not have written his own death and burial account. He cites Genesis 12:6 which uses the phrase "while the Canaanites were in the land." During Moses' lifetime, the Canaanites were never not in the land, and it was not until the conquest of Joshua's day that they began to be removed, thus Hobbes declares that Moses could not have written this passage. Further, Numbers 21:14 references the Book of the Wars of the Lord, which Hobbes reckons to be the writings of Moses, and thus Numbers was written after Moses' lifetime. Hobbes does not intend to demolish the authority of the text, however, as he indicates that all that Moses is said to have said he did indeed say, thus the text is not dishonest, Moses just

---

[46] Ibid.: 181.
[47] Ibid.
[48] Thomas Hobbes, Leviathan, Richard Tuck, ed., (Cambridge, UK: Cambridge University Press), 260-268.

did not author all that tradition assigns to him.

While Hobbes' motive was not to redefine God, Benedict Spinoza's was. He emphasized the immanence of God, holding that God was monistic and impersonal, and that he was revealed in the laws of nature and was to be understood by reason. Spinoza's critical method is apparent in his *Tractatus Theologico Politicus* (1670), and is characterized by a threefold hermeneutic process, which assumed that scriptures should be studied in the same way as would nature: in light of reason. First, he focused on the linguistic analysis of the time of writing. This involved in-depth analysis of the Hebrew text and developments in the Hebrew language itself. Second, he promoted topical and systematic organizations of the text under headers, so that as interlocutors interpret they have other similar and related passages at their disposal. Finally, he concentrated heavily on the method of textual formation. This constituted his primary achievement in Biblical criticism as he considered the author's context, setting, motivation, limitation, education, and a host of other factors. Spinoza made textual formation a critical step in the process of ascertaining what the text meant.

As a result of his investigation Spinoza rejected Mosaic authorship in light of what he considered retrospective passages and anachronism. He asserted that the Pentateuch, along with Joshua and Judges were the work of later redactors, including Ezra the scribe. Spinoza likewise considered Nehemiah to have been penned possibly in the second century B.C., Proverbs to have been post-exilic, Chronicles to have been so unreliable as to be undeserving of being included in the canon, Jeremiah to have been the product of plural authorship, Job to have been initially a gentile poem, and Daniel to have been inauthentic.[49] Spinoza identified two kinds of scriptures. First, prophetic theology, which was beyond reason and could be understood only from the scriptures themselves. Of the second category – narrative – Spinoza was highly critical. He perceived the writers of narrative to have gravely mischaracterized God as essentially a secondary cause rather than the immediate efficient cause. Spinoza argued against the dualism of God and nature, suggesting there was no dichotomy and no distinction: God and nature are one. Thus Spinoza also argued there is no beginning or end, no teleological – no purpose, and no cause; and thus his Biblical criticism led to (or was built upon) a significant redefinition of God. In light of Spinoza's conclusions, Bratton credits him as having immeasurable impact on the modern understanding of the Bible, particularly in his showing "that the Bible is not one book but many, coming from different periods of history and exhibiting different degrees of inspiration.[50] [emphasis mine]

Spinoza's conclusion that the text is not univocal is of particular importance in the context of the present discussion, and if the argument is to made for univocality and consequently for the authority of the text, then Spinoza's criticisms cannot be ignored.

Richard Simon wrote from Paris in 1678 his Histoire Critique de Vieux Testament, which he published as a more complete version seven years later. His Critique consisted of three books, the first was a Biblical criticism, focusing on Jewish historical methods and Mosaic authorship; the second was an account of the various Old Testament translations (he relied on

---

[49] Bratton: 183.
[50] Ibid.: 184.

the Masoretic text and the Greek Septuagint, perceiving previous Hebrew Old Testament manuscripts so obscure as to make sola scripture untenable); and the third was an account of the major Old Testament commentators. Additionally, he completed three New Testament critiques, but for all his labor his primary unique achievement was in his theory that throughout Jewish history, there was a tradition of historical recording and a continuous succession of historians who fulfilled this task. Simon hypothesized that it was from this group that Moses and other Biblical writers borrowed.[51]

Jean Astruc wrote his *Conjectures sur la Genèse* in 1753 to counter, in particular, Hobbes' and Spinoza's critiques of Biblical reliability. Astruc used contemporary methods, including those of Eichhorn and Wilhelm de Wette (father of the historical critical school) in order to offer a Biblical criticism of his own. He focused on doublets (retellings of historical narratives) and the stylistic distinctions between passages that named God as YHWH and those that titled him Elohim, and concluded thusly that there were two authors of Genesis (one of whom was Moses).[52] In so doing, he laid the groundwork for Wellhausen's documentary hypothesis which would be forthcoming over a hundred years later.

Julius Wellhausen proposed his documentary theory in his *Prolegomena zur Geschichte Israels*. Built on Astruc's considerations of stylistic distinctions, Wellhausen's hypothesis is referred to as the JEDP theory, an acronym for the distinctive writers that Wellhausen perceived to be involved in the initial

---

[51] Louis Wallis: 43.
[52] Ana M. Acosta, "Conjectures and Speculations: Jean Astruc, Obstetrics, and Biblical Criticism in Eighteenth Century France" in Eighteenth-Century Studies, Vol. 35, No. 2 (Winter, 2002): 257-259.

transmission of the text. The J is for the Jahwist (JHVH the Latinized transliteration of YHWH), the E is for the Elohist, the D is for the deuteronomist or the redactor – perhaps the one responsible for the many doublets, and P is for the priestly writer who penned Leviticus, etc. Wallis describes Wellhausen's critique as so influential that "Bible study everywhere took a new start."[53]

Thus Hobbes' critiques find their fulfillment in Wellhausen's theory, and ultimately the prescriptive value of the text, under this theory, as anything more than a cultural and (somewhat) historical commentary can be legitimately questioned. While the approach answers one prong of Locke's fork,[54] in so doing it ultimately undermines the authority of the text. Still, Biblical criticism advanced beyond Wellhausen, Against the backdrop of World War I, Willis interprets the role of Biblical criticism in the context of social development. In particular, Wallis sees the Biblical text – despite the allegations launched against it by the textual critics – as a fundamental cog in the development of a new social consciousness which would light the way, via a democratic mindset (removing interpretive power from the autocracy and passing it along to the people), for that war-torn generation to "move onward through the flames of war"[55] into a brighter era. Wallis' optimism carries with it an internal contradiction that is notable. He suggests that we need not orthodoxy but "a conservatism that maintains all the religious values enshrined in the Scriptures,"[56] yet the Biblical

---

[53] Wallis: 46.
[54] Either the text is completely and equally inspired or not. Wellhausen's theory concludes it is not, and consequently begs the question of the Bible's ethical value.
[55] Wallis: 49.
[56] Ibid.

criticism which he lauds creates a condition in which the boundaries between truth and falsity in a propositional sense are blurred at best. W.R. Taylor diagnoses the problem, and attempts a prescription, and in so doing really only illustrates the problem. He suggests, "we should be ready to abandon the indefensible and to concentrate our attention on the essential qualities of the sacred oracles as time and research bring them into fuller relief."[57] Taylor's assessment invites several questions. Which values should be maintained, and which discarded? Which are indefensible and which are essential? Without a propositional approach – such as that employed by James Nash – this is a question impossible to answer with any certainty. Taylor suggests that Biblical criticism has resulted in the demise of "the belief in verbal inspiration, the inerrancy of the Bible in all its parts in science and history, and its infallibility in morals and religion,"[58] and that better conceptions of God are now possible. Taylor's observation, though it seeks to redeem the text from its captors, represents a supreme degree of inconsistency that requires a greater degree of faith to bear than is required for accepting the legitimacy of the text as a whole. He suggests the Bible is not revelation but is simply the record of it.[59] But where does the revelation end and the record begin? Taylor argues that though old ideas of what constitutes suitable warrant for authority have passed away, what has emerged should instill confidence in the reader:

In short, we can say that recent research has brought into

---

[57] W.R. Taylor, "Biblical Criticism and Modern Faith" in The Journal of Religion, Vol. 23, No. 4 (Oct., 1943): 229.
[58] Ibid.:230.
[59] Ibid.: 231.

high relief (a) the Bible's unique significance in the cultural process, (b) the qualitative superiority of the Biblical literature comparatively, and (c) the Bible as a body of sincere and vital documents.[60]

Though his three ideas here are commonly held, the issue of whether the text is worthy of confidence remains disputed, perhaps in part due to a pervasive inattention to detail on the part of textual-authority-apologists as illustrated further by Taylor's culminating exhortation: "we must be careful to show that the essential truths which we by our methods reach in the Scriptures can and must be made meaningful to our generation."[61] Unfortunately for Taylor's thesis, this generation – like any other – may have difficulty accepting essential truths from a source whose apparently non-essential ones are not truths at all. It seems, then, only consistent (consistency being an important and deciding factor, in my estimation) to either abandon ideas of revelation altogether, and consequently the optimism and even the supposedly better conceptions of God derived from the text if the text itself is devalued, and dismiss the values enshrined in the text as not being suitably warranted from the text, or alternately to consider the text in a prima facie way – interpreting it in the most plain or natural sense – and in response we may consider the value of the content based upon not only the individual parts but also upon the sum of those parts. Such a consideration is not foreign to those represented in the Bible, and seems to be the expected response the writers

---

[60] Ibid.: 239-240.
[61] Ibid.: 240.

sought from their readers.⁶²

That Moses wrote the first five books, for example, is the representation of the Bible itself and is attested to by earliest interpretive tradition. Joshua 8:31-32 distinguishes between the law of Moses (v.32) and the book of the law of Moses (v. 31), as the law generally referenced the entire body of the covenantal stipulations – including all six-hundred and thirteen commandments (the *mizvot*), and was usually represented by the first ten.⁶³ Forms of the phrase book of the law (ספר התורה) are used some twenty-one times in the Hebrew Bible,⁶⁴ and notably the term does not appear until the concluding chapters of Moses' final book. The term is later applied by Jesus (Mk. 20:26) when he references events in Exodus as being contained in the book of Moses (τῇ βίβλῳ Μωϋσέως⁶⁵) and as "Scripture." Jesus directly recognized Exodus,⁶⁶ Leviticus,⁶⁷ Numbers⁶⁸ and Deuteronomy⁶⁹ all to be Mosaic, and referenced Genesis as genuine and legitimately included in the Hebrew Bible.⁷⁰

---

⁶² I argue elsewhere that the hermeneutic utilized nearly exclusively by Biblical characters was a plain or natural sense approach. See Christopher Cone, *Prolegomena On Biblical Hermeneutics and Method:* (Fort Worth, TX: Tyndale Seminary Press, 2015), 111-118.
⁶³ It was probably this shorter list that Joshua wrote on the stones in the events of Joshua 8.
⁶⁴ Deut. 28:58; 28:61; 29:20; 30:10; 31:24; 31:26; Josh. 8:31; 8:34; 23:6; 24:26; 2 Kin. 14:6; 22:8; 22:11; 23:24; 2 Chron. 17:9; 34:14, 15; Neh. 8:1, 3, 18; 9:3.
⁶⁵ NA28, 131.
⁶⁶ Cf., Mk. 7:10 and Ex. 20:12; also Mk. 12:26 and Ex. 3:6.
⁶⁷ Cf., Mt. 8:4 and Lev. 13:49; 14:2ff.
⁶⁸ Cf., Jn. 3:14 and Num. 21:9.
⁶⁹ Cf., Mt. 19:7-8 and Deut. 24:1-4.
⁷⁰ Timothy Lin catalogs Jesus' affirmations as follows: "He confirmed the genuineness of the first two chapters of Genesis by testifying to the creation of Adam and Eve as a historical fact, and not a myth or legend (Matt. 19:4-6; Mark 10:5-9). When He rebuked the scribes and

Not only did Jesus consider Genesis genuine, but he also considered it Mosaic. He refers to the Hebrew Bible as "the Law of Moses and the Prophets, and the Psalms" (Lk. 24:44, NASB), a structural parallel to the Masoretic text of Torah (law), Nevi'im (prophets), and Ketuvim (writings, of which Psalms is the first book). Also, in Luke 11:49-51 Jesus details a chronology of martyred prophets from the foundation of the world to that point. He references Abel as the first and Zechariah as the last. Abel's death occurs in Genesis – the first book of the Tanakh, and Zechariah's in Chronicles – the final book of the Tanakh. It seems rather certain that Jesus understood the entire Hebrew Bible to be genuine, and the individual books it contained to be organized as we observe in the Masoretic text. He understood that the Law (or Book of the Law) of Moses – the Torah – was both genuine and Mosaic.

But what of Wellhausen's refined multi-author theory? Emblematic of an influential tradition of Biblical scholarship, Timothy Lin challenges the documentary hypothesis as fallacious and unworkable.[71] With detailed consideration of

---

Pharisees, He mentioned "the blood of Abel" as the beginning of the Jews' guilt (Matt. 23:35). He confirmed that Noah's flood was a historical destruction (Matt. 24:37-39) and the devastation of Sodom and Gomorrah as God's judgment (Matt. 11:23-24). He described Lot's time in Sodom and the judgment of his wife as a historical warning regarding the last days (Luke 17:28-32). In His preaching and teaching, He often spoke of Abraham (John 8:37-40,56-58) and repeatedly He testified of Abraham, Isaac, and Jacob (Mark 12:26) and their lives before God (Matt. 8:11; 22:32). The above references indicate that Christ testified to the truthfulness of essentially the entire book of Genesis. (Timothy Lin, Genesis: A Biblical Theology, 4th ed., (Carmel, IN: Biblical Studies Ministries International, 2002), 29-30.).

[71] Lin's critique is potent and worthy of consideration here: "This hypothesis is far from being workable. For instance, in certain J passages "Elohim," which is characteristic of E, is present (3:1,3,5; 4:25;

internal problems with the hypothesis, Lin argues that the analytic method the textual critics purport to use is not being consistently applied to these passages and that a consistent application of the method would not provide grounding for the multi-author conclusion. Gary Rendsburg critiques the theory on grounds that it fails to account for chiastic structure and other parallels found in the text,[72] though his argument is dismissed by Marc Brettler who believes Rendsburg's assertions fail to adequately resolve all the issues the multi-authorship theory raises.[73] The worthy considerations by both writers are emblematic of the present debate regarding the conclusiveness of the multi-author theory – to be precise, regarding what is the

---

7:9,16; 9:27; and so on), and in certain E and P passages "Yahweh," which is characteristic of J, is found (17:1; 22:11; and so on). In order to cover this embarrassing situation, the critics cut some verses and clauses out of their context and assigned them to another document. They cut 5:29 out of P and assigned it to J, because the divine name "Yahweh" (which is translated "the LORD") is present. Yet they left 4:25 in J although "Elohim" is in this verse. They separated 7:16b that has "Yahweh" from the midst of P and assigned it to J. However, they left 9:26 and 16:13 undivided in J, but both have "Yahweh" and "Elohim." Genesis 21:1 is a dilemma to the critics because both clauses have "Yahweh." According to their theory of "doublets" they should separate them. Yet according to their usage of divine names to designate different authors, they have to place the couplets together. To cut the knot they assigned 21:1a to J and 21:1b to P. How absurd! Genesis 21:33 was assigned to J, disregarding the presence of "Elohim" in 33b. Genesis 22:11,14 are both assigned to E, yet both have "Yahweh." Genesis 28:21 is assigned to E, yet "Yahweh" is also found there. These examples are sufficient to show the fallacy of this hypothesis." (Lin, 27-28).

[72] Gary A. Rendsburg, The Redaction of Genesis (Winona Lake, IN: Eisenbraun, 1986), 104ff.

[73] Marc Brettler, "Rendsburg's 'The Redaction of Genesis'" in The Jewish Quarterly Review, New Series, Vol. 78, No. 1/2 (Jul. - Oct. 1987): 113-119.

genuine product of the critical method, the matter is unresolved.

Benjamin Mazar understood Genesis to be "a monumental historiographic composition, the product of rich and variegated material collected, combined, arranged, and worked into one harmonious tract, with the purpose of portraying both the beginnings of mankind and the origins of Israel in the spirit of the monotheistic concept, and with a didactic aim."[74] Mazar, not unlike Umberto Cassuto, based his criticism of Mosaic authorship not on literary form but on a number of historical factors he recognized as anachronisms in the text and which he believed pointed to a much later date than the roughly 1400 BC/BCE date demanded in the text itself.[75] His thesis is seemingly based in large part on a presupposition that there is no (divinely inspired) prophetic utterance (i.e., that the Hebrew prophets were not speaking on God's behalf and that there is no legitimate divine revelation). Note the following phrases used by Mazar: "it is within reason" (used twice),[76] "it is then in place to assume,"[77] "[O]ne may, apparently, also count among these...,"[78] "it seems to me,"[79] "in my view, it is much more within reason,"[80] "[O]ne may find in the accounts...,"[81] "there is

---

[74] Benjamin Mazar, "The Historical Background of the Book of Genesis" in Journal of Near Eastern Studies, Vol. 28, No. 2 (Apr. 1969): 74.
[75] Mazar says, "It is within reason that Genesis was given its original written form during the time when the Davidic empire was being established, and that the additions and supplements of later authors were only intended to help bridge the time gap for contemporary readers, and had no decisive effect on its contents of its overall character." (Mazar: 74).
[76] Ibid.:74.
[77] Ibid.:75.
[78] Ibid.:76.
[79] Ibid.
[80] Ibid.:77.
[81] Ibid.:78.

no need...to assign it a later date."[82] Conjecture seems to play a significant role in his assertions.

He also suggests that the ethnographic similarities between Genesis 16 and Psalm 83 (the date of which he says is reasonably understood to be during the end of the period of the Judges) suggest a later date for Genesis.[83] He notes that the characteristics of the Joseph account "are such as to make us think that the traditions and motifs joined together in this single tableau...were given their sophisticated novelistic literary form no earlier than the beginning of the Monarchy."[84] Perhaps most notably, though, he argues that the Genesis 49:10 blessing of Judah was not prophetic, but that it was a later developed apologetic for Judah's right to rule – a right that is prominently featured and defended during the early monarchy period. While this is a significant instance of assumed anachronism (as there seems no other basis for it other than the non-prophetic presupposition), aside from these numerous defenses of Davidic kingship Mazar cites several alleged anachronisms in Genesis. Notably, in context, most are related to Davidic right, and one might wonder if these would be anachronisms at all if Davidic right was indeed a product of prophetic utterance. Nonetheless, these would need to be addressed by any who would defend an early date consistent with Mosaic authorship, and Mazar suggests (without, in this context, any particular explanation of why) that those who have attempted to resolve these issues in light of various external sources (such as Akkadian sources, Mari documents, Nuzi tablets, and variously dated Egyptian

---

[82] Ibid.:78.
[83] Ibid.:79.
[84] Ibid.:82-83.

sources) have "gone too far,"[85] though he admits that there is "certainly room for thought and reconsideration of the conflicting views as to the dating of the "patriarchal period" to the first, second, and third quarters of the second millennium B.C."[86]

In short, Mazar's conclusions are not presented as necessary, though he does (of course) prefer them to the alternative. In any case, it is at least clear from Mazar's writing that – as is the case with the JEPD hypothesis – the late-date theory is far from a certitude. Also, it would seem that the late-date theory and JEPD seem grounded in the presupposition that divine revelation and prophetic utterance are not legitimate possibilities here.

Paul Minear recognizes the challenges that Biblical criticism faces in light of presuppositions and first principles.[87] Minear suggests, quoting Croce, that in this epoch the prevailing frame of reference – "The heart and brain (of recent historiography)...is naturalism."[88] This pre-commitment to naturalism provides a set of guidelines that cannot be easily

---

[85] Ibid.: 76.
[86] Ibid.: 76.
[87] Minear observes that, "The reflective historian must consciously orient his technical research with an articulate "frame of reference," a view of history which determines his presuppositions, defines his method and circumscribes his conclusions. Such orientation is particularly important in an epoch when perspectives of thought shift so rapidly. Each successive change in world-view stimulates new conceptions of history, raises new questions for the historian to answer, and provokes new assaults upon prevailing methodology." (Paul S. Minear, "How Objective is Biblical Criticism" in Journal of Bible and Religion, Vol. 9, No. 4 (Nov., 1941): 217.)
[88] Minear: 218.

discarded.[89] In particular, Minear suggests that Biblical historians (few of whom are "avowed naturalists"[90]) utilize a method which is grown from and at least implies naturalism. What fruit then is to be expected from a naturalistically based method? Certainly the tension between an assumed metaphysic and a method which negates the metaphysic is not conducive to a high degree of consistency in the end. Yet it is this tension that Locke (for example) acknowledges as present in the discussion.

Considering, for example, the Deuteronomy 34 account of Moses' death, we note that Hobbes perceives this to be evidence against Mosaic authorship of the Pentateuch as a unit, yet there are two possibilities worthy of consideration and which may present a resolution to the issue: (1) If this was indeed revelation, rather than the mere product of human invention, then theoretically God could have informed Moses of what would occur. Predictive prophecy (if such a possibility is allowed for) accounts for nearly a third of the Hebrew Bible (if a plain or natural sense hermeneutic is consistently applied). To dismiss off-hand the possibility of divine revelation seems more grounded in naturalistic presuppositions and an intention to demythologize the Bible than in evenhanded textual criticism. (2) Nonetheless, it is not a necessity for genuineness that Moses wrote his own obituary. That there might have been a separate writer (Joshua, perhaps) who wrote the Deuteronomy epilogue would not negate Mosaic authorship of the Pentateuch as a unit

---

[89] Minear suggests that, "The historian's function is to establish generalizations applicable at all times and places. The test of his conclusions is their predictive accuracy. Novelty, particularity, becomes a scandal. Confronted by the unique, the historian can only stutter, "It can't be!" Thus the history that is dictated by a naturalistic world-view ends by negating itself." (Minear: 218.).
[90] Minear: 219.

- much in the same way that Jesus' reference to the Ketuvim (the Writings section of the Hebrew Bible) as "the Psalms" did not imply that the book of Psalms was the only component of the Ketuvim, and in the same way that we refer to the Epistle to the Romans as Pauline, though it claims, in fact, to have been penned by Tertius (as Paul's amanuensis).[91] The internal evidence of the Hebrew (OT) and Greek (NT) texts considered collectively leaves no doubt that if the texts are themselves genuine, they argue for genuineness and Mosaic authorship of Genesis. The early external evidence likewise introduces no doubt.

The second-century BC pseudo-epigraphical Book of Jubilees presents a creation account similar (though not identical) to that of Genesis, but unlike Genesis, Jubilees contains a preface affirming the authorship of the creation story.[92] The Jubilees account not only asserts Mosaic authorship, but narrates how he came to write the creation account. In similar fashion, Philo of Alexandria, a notable first-century AD Jewish philosopher, understood Genesis to be of Mosaic origin, extolling, for example, the philosophic prowess Moses demonstrated in beginning his laws with a creation account.[93] That Philo recognized Mosaic authorship is important

---

[91] Romans 16:22.
[92] Jubilees 2:1 reads as follows, "And the angel of the presence spake to Moses according to the word of the Lord, saying: "Write all the words of the creation, how in six days the Lord God finished all His works and all that he created, and rested on the Sabbath day and hallowed it for all ages, and appointed it as a sign for all His works." (R. H. Charles, "A New Translation of the Book of Jubilees. Part I" in The Jewish Quarterly Review, Vol. 6, No. 1 (Oct., 1893): 187.).
[93] Philo's comments are as follows: "But Moses...made the beginning of his laws entirely beautiful, and in all respects admirable, neither at once declaring what ought to be done or the contrary, nor (since it was

not just in light of his philosophical assessment of Moses' motivations, but also because Philo was a pioneer of Biblical criticism. He was an important developer of the allegorical hermeneutic he frequently utilized in order to resolve aspects of the text that he perceived to be inconsistent with the Hellenistic philosophy of his day. Philo, it would seem, did not consider Mosaic authorship to be troublesome at all. On the contrary, he considered it to be an important fact, and one that connected cosmology with ethical theory.

Though his objectivity as a historian has been questioned,[94] Josephus nonetheless offers an important first-century AD Jewish perspective on many aspects of Israel's history. He discusses (in similar fashion to Philo) Moses' unique approach to legislation, recognizing the acumen with which Moses turns minds to God before turning their attention to

---

necessary to mould beforehand the dispositions of those who were to use his laws) inventing fables himself or adopting those which had been invented by others. And his exordium, as I have already said, is most admirable; embracing the creation of the world, under the idea that the law corresponds to the world and the world to the law, and that a man who is obedient to the law, being, by so doing, a citizen of the world, arranges his actions with reference to the intention of nature, in harmony with which the whole universal world is regulated...Since, then, this world is visible and the object of our external senses, it follows of necessity that it must have been created; on which account it was not without a wise purpose that he recorded its creation, giving a very venerable account of God...And he says that the world was made in six days.." (emphasis mine) (Philo, "On the Creation" in The Works of Philo, C.D. Yonge, ed. (Peabody, MA: Hendrickson, 1993), 3.).

[94] For a thoroughgoing discussion of Josephus' apologetic designs, see Louis H. Feldman, "Josephus' Portrait of Moses" in The Jewish Quarterly Review, New Series, Vol. 82, No. 3/4 (Jan. - Apr. 1992): 285-328.

laws.[95] He also speaks of the creation account as being entirely Mosaic.[96] In summarizing verse-by-verse the Genesis 1 creation account, Josephus asserts Mosaic authorship no less than four times ("Moses said," 1:1:29; "Moses says," 1:1:33; "Moses...begins to talk philosophically," 1:1:34; and "Moses says further," 1:1:37).[97]

Josephus, Philo, and the Book of Jubilees represent early external evidence complementing the Biblical assertions of Mosaic authorship of Genesis, and they are not inconsistent with more recent views. Moses Maimonides (twelfth century), for example, was unapologetic about Mosaic authorship. He includes as one of his Thirteen Principles the following: "I believe with perfect faith that the entire Torah that we have now is that which was given to Moses."[98] One mainstream contemporary Jewish encyclopedia argues in favor of singular authorship and challenges certain premises of the documentary hypothesis, including alleged anachronisms, historiographic

---

[95] Josephus says, "Now when Moses was desirous to teach this lesson to his countrymen, he did not begin the establishment of his laws after the same manner that other legislators did; I mean, upon contracts and other rites between one man and another, but by raising their minds upwards to regard God, and his creation of the world; and by persuading them, that we men are the most excellent of the creatures of God upon the earth." (Flavius Josephus, The Works of Josephus Complete and Unabridged, William Whiston, trans., (Peabody, MA: Hendrickson, 1987), Antiquities, Preface, 21.).

[96] Josephus comments briefly here, "I shall now betake myself to the history before me, after I have first mentioned what Moses says of the creation of the world, which I find described in the sacred books after the manner following." (Josephus, Antiquities, Preface, 26.).

[97] Josephus, Antiquities, 1:1:29-37.

[98] Moses Maimonides, Commentary on the Mishnah, Tractate Sanhedrin, trans. by Fred Rosner (New York, NY: Sepher- Hermon Press, 1981), ch.11, principle 8.

principles, and doublets.[99] Furthermore, the encyclopedia directly counters textual criticism on seven points: (1) there is no external proof of compilation; (2) interpretations of so-called internal evidence to that end is "unstable and deceptive;" (3) the process leading to the compilation conclusion is complex beyond consistency; (4) even if alleged contradictions and repetitions existed, they would not prove plural authorship, just as this process applied to other single author works would be met with equal failure; (5) the theory is unnecessary and based on multiple misunderstandings of ideas, tendencies, and themes; (6) arguments based on variations of language are circular; and (7) exegetical mishandling is necessary for the compilation understanding.[100]

Though the internal and external evidence presented here may not satisfy some readers of the certainty of Mosaic authorship, perhaps there has been shown enough evidence to warrant reasonable consideration of the mere possibility that Genesis is genuinely Mosaic. If the reader is willing to grant this much, then the possibility that the text provides some binding ethical grounding remains. If not, then the discussion needs move no further, as the Bible would offer nothing of any real ethical value beyond what one might expect from a fable or a legend. As Isaac Abravanel argues, if the Biblical text (and the Torah in particular) is presumed to be authoritative, then it

---

[99] Jewishencyclopedia.com asserts, "Anachronisms such as various critics allege in Genesis do not in reality exist; and their assumption is based on a misunderstanding of the historiographic principles of the book...Nor are there any repetitions or unnecessary doublets." (Benno Jacob and Emil Hirsch, "Genesis, The Book of" in Jewish encyclopedia.com, sections 12-35, viewed 1/30/2010.).
[100] Jacob and Hirsch, "Genesis, The Book of," section 35.

must be believed in its entirety and not doubted.[101] To assert that the Genesis account is not genuine requires that one dismiss its ethical contribution as non-binding. Thus, if we would view the book as binding we must consider it to be genuine, and if we cannot assent to this, we may merely rely on Callicott's warning not to miss the point that many Jews and Christians consult the Biblical text for ethical guidance.[102] We find, then, that the text is either ethically binding, or at least a significant number of people perceive that it is – whether with proper warrant or not – and those people will seek to follow the meaningful advice found within its pages. As Henry Morris reminds us, Genesis is the foundation of all the Biblical books, and is thus the most critical piece of the book "that has exerted the greatest influence on history of any book ever produced."[103]

---

[101] Abravanel suggests, "...it is not proper to postulate principles for the divine Torah, nor foundations in the matter of beliefs, for we are obligated to believe everything that is written in the Torah. We are not permitted to doubt even the smallest thing in it..." (Isaac Abravanel, Principles of Faith, Rosh Amanah, Menachem Kellner, trans., (Oxford, UK: Littman Library of Jewish Civilization, 2000), 195.).

[102] J. Baird Callicott reminds us that, "Contemporary Jews and Christians, searching for meaningful advice about how to live in the world in which today they find themselves, will consult the Bible and will inevitably ponder what they read (in translation) in light of their contemporary concerns, their personal experience, and their own locale." (Contemporary Jews and Christians, searching for meaningful advice about how to live in the world in which today they find themselves, will consult the Bible and will inevitably ponder what they read (in translation) in light of their contemporary concerns, their personal experience, and their own locale." (J. Baird Callicott, "Genesis Revisited: Murian Musings on the Lynn White, Jr. Debate" in Environmental History Review, Vol. 14, No 1/2, 1989 Conference Papers, Part Two (Spring-Summer, 1990): 85.).

[103] Henry M. Morris, The Genesis Record: A Scientific and Devotional Commentary on the Book of Beginnings (Grand Rapids, MI: Baker Book House, 1976), 17.

7
PRIORITY OF BIBLICAL HERMENEUTICS OVER THEOLOGICAL SYSTEMS

A theological system ought to be the product of exegetical study of Scripture, not a preface to exegetical work. Hermeneutical principles are first observed in the Scriptures themselves, even in a cursory and casual reading. Those principles are then applied in actual study of the text in the exegetical process.

This important order of principles and process is one reason that references to a "dispensational hermeneutic" is an inconsistency. Dispensational thinkers claim that they (are at least attempting to) consistently apply a literal grammatical historical hermeneutic to the Biblical text. In that hermeneutic approach, dispensational conclusions are just that – conclusions. If we claim to hold to a dispensational hermeneutic, then on the one hand we are asserting our lack of bias in consistently applying an *objective* hermeneutic, while on the other we are showing our bias by claiming a dispensational presupposition. One can't have it both ways. Dispensationalists have struggled with this to some degree. Reformed theologians, on the other hand, have virtually dismissed this issue altogether.

For example, Kevin DeYoung suggests that our theological system should not only inform our exegesis, but that our theological system should tell us how to exegete.[104] DeYoung's definition of exegesis is a good one that both Reformed and Dispensational interlocutors would accept:

> Exegesis is what you do when you look at a single text of Scripture and try to understand what the author–speaking in a specific culture, addressing to a specific audience, writing for a specific purpose–intended to communicate.

But how would one's systematic theology effect one's exegesis? Part of the problem is in affirming a historical distinction between Biblical scholarship and theology. I reject the independence of those two disciplines and affirm the dependence of one on the other. If one is not strong in the Scriptures, they are not well equipped for making theological claims. Theological aptitude does not make for better exegesis, but it does make for better applications (which should follow strong exegesis).

I would go so far as to assert that not only should exegesis inform systematic theology, it should be the absolute governing principle in deriving systematic theology. L.S. Chafer once defined systematic theology as "the collecting, systematically arranging, comparing, exhibiting, and defending all facts concerning God and his works from any and every source."[105] That definition is in my estimation, far too broad. In Chafer's (otherwise solid) approach, the systematic theology is being

---

[104] Kevin De Young, "Your Theology Should Tell You How to Exegete" at *The Gospel Coalition,* February 23, 2012. Viewed at https://www.thegospelcoalition.org/blogs/kevin-deyoung/your-theological-system-should-tell-you-how-to-exegete/.

[105] Lewis Sperry Chafer, *Systematic Theology, Vol I* (Dallas, TX: Dallas Theological Seminary, 1947), 6.

derived from extra-Biblical sources as well as Biblical, and thus one cannot have a certainty that they have understood the data correctly – or even identified the data at all. If systematic theology is derived exclusively from Scripture, on the other hand, then the level of certainty regarding conclusions increases dramatically.

DeYoung suggests that "systematic theology looks at the whole Bible and tries to understand all that God says on a given subject..." While DeYoung's definition is stronger than Chafer's (as DeYoung's implies the Bible is the sole source of data), DeYoung's conclusion seems to contradict the initial definition, when he says that,

> As a Christian I hope that my theology is open to correction, but as a minister I have to start somewhere. We all do. For me that means starting with Reformed theology and my confessional tradition and sticking with that unless I have really good reason not to.[106]

DeYoung begins with Reformed Theology and the confessional tradition, and reads the Bible through that lens. That is, in effect, reading extra-Biblical systematized theology into the text. The danger is twofold: (1) if the systematic theology is not exclusively and comprehensively Biblical (even the most Biblical of Reformed theologians would admit that there is some reading between the lines in Reformed doctrines and confessions), then extra-Biblical data is read into the Bible; (2) reading broad contexts into more narrow ones can inhibit understanding of authorial intent. Certainly, we need to consider theological

---

[106] Kevin DeYoung, Ibid.

context in understanding a passage, but that theological context is drawn from the text itself, and in consideration of near Biblical context first. Allowing a theological system to help determine exegesis is not exegesis at all – it is eisegesis (at least insofar as the theology impacts the reading). By definition, exegesis is drawing out the meaning of the text, while eisegesis reads meaning into the text.

DeYoung admits that we must have a systematic theology in order to understand specific contexts, suggesting that we cannot properly exegete the text without a pre-formed theological system. He asks rhetorically,

> Without a systematic theology how can you begin to know what to do with the eschatology of Ezekiel or the sacramental language in John 6 or the psalmist's insistence that he is righteous and blameless?[107]

This is eisegesis. To read a theology or a tradition into a passage is not an appropriate way to understand authorial intent in the narrow context. The broader context (of a book, for example) is made up of smaller units of context (pericopes, etc.). One must understand what the smaller units are saying in order to correctly assess the broader units. Once the smaller units have been assessed, we can make assessments of the broader. This reflects the interplay of narrow and broad *textual* contexts – but that is very different from reading a theological system (which in DeYoung's case is Reformed and confessional) into the text.

---

[107] Ibid.

Rather than begin with any tradition or theology, why not simply read the passages, assess them in light of normal hermeneutic principles (literal grammatical historical), and allow the passages to speak for themselves? Why not then simply apply the narrow context to the broader context?

Reformed theology cannot do this in some cases, because the theological results would contradict the system. This is illustrated vividly in DeYoung's handling of the 144,000 in Revelation 7.[108] DeYoung asserts these are stylized and allegorical references that cannot logically refer to an actual number of ethnically Jewish people. If these references were to be understood literally, then there would have to be an admission of a future physical and spiritual restoration of ethnic Israel – an insurmountable monkey wrench in the Reformed eschatology. Likewise, if the eschatology of Ezekiel is taken at face value and interpreted in a straightforward manner, then the interpreter is faced with the same monkey wrench: there is a future in God's covenant plan for ethnic Israel in the land which He promised to the nation. These cases illustrate how imperative it is for Reformed theology to read its system into the text, for without doing so, the system is rendered incoherent by the exegetical data.

The bottom line is a simple one: we either submit to authorial intent regardless of the theological outcomes (recognizing that theology is an outcome, not a starting place), or we pursue an affirmation of a predetermined theological system with which we can be content. One is submissive to the

---

[108] Kevin DeYoung, "Theological Primer: The 144,000" at The gospel Coalition, April 28, 2017, viewed at https://www.thegospelcoalition.org/blogs/kevin-deyoung/theological-primer-the-144000/.

Writer, the other is not. At times, both Reformed and Dispensational thinkers have found themselves in various places between these two points. The challenge for any student of the Bible is to be consistent in our pursuit of submission to the Author, in acknowledgment of authorial intent.

8
PRIORITY OF OLD TESTAMENT LITERALISM IN NEW TESTAMENT USAGE:
JOHANNINE PARALLELISM OF FORESHADOWING AND FULFILLMENT[109]

Introduction

Two nuanced views are discernible in *classic dispensationalist* understanding of the New Testament (NT) use of the Old Testament (OT), and are well represented by Robert Thomas' Inspired *Sensus Plenior* Application (ISPA) and David Cooper's Law of Double Reference (LDR) concepts. These two explanatory devices argue that seemingly non-literal interpretations of OT prophecy by NT authors do in fact fit within the framework of literal grammatical historical understanding. While both are plausible and have significant advantages, their limitations may point us to another device (referred to here as the Johannine Parallelism of Foreshadowing and Fulfillment [JPFF]) in order to more strongly affirm that the NT use of the OT is indeed rooted in and consistent with the literal grammatical historical method (LGH).

---

[109] Originally presented to the Council on Dispensational Hermeneutics, as "Johannine Parallelism of Foreshadowing and Fulfillment: Affirming the New Testament Use of Old Testament Prophecy as Uncompromisingly Literal," September 14, 2016.

The JPFF device is most readily observed in John's Gospel, and particular in his usage of *fulfillment* language and *sign* metaphor. It is evident that the Johannine concept of fulfillment *is more consistently the culmination of foreshadowing than it is the simple occurrence of predicted events.* While sharing important advantages of ISPA and LDR, JPFF is also promising in that it addresses the most significant difficulty shared by ISPA and LDR, and in so doing may provide a stronger affirmation that the NT use of the OT is fully compatible with the literal grammatical historical hermeneutic.

An appendix follows these considerations, drawing brief comparison to three *non-classic dispensationalist* approaches to determine whether JPFF is to be preferred over the three models, and if so on what basis.

Two Respected Platforms:
Thomas' Inspired *Sensus Plenior* Application
And Cooper's Law of Double Reference

Dr. Robert Thomas suggests that when we understand the OT and NT through the lens of LGH, we discover two kinds of uses by the NT of the OT.[110] In the first application, the NT writer employs LGH and goes no further. In the second, the NT writer goes beyond simple LGH to give an ISPA.[111] Thomas reassures that ISPA neither grants contemporary interpreters license to copy the methodology of NT writers, nor violates the principle of single meaning. Further it does not compromise the literal meaning of the OT passage, but simply applies the OT

---

[110] Robert L. Thomas, "The New Testament Use of the Old Testament," in *The Masters Seminary Journal*, 13/1, Spring 2002: 79-98.
[111] Ibid.: 79.

wording to a new setting."¹¹² Still, the ISPA view seems problematic in that it admits nonliteral application of the OT by the NT. Thomas describes and addresses the problem as follows:

> Does not the NT's assigning of an application based on a second meaning to an OT passage violate that principle? That the passage has two meanings is obvious, but only one of those meanings derives from a grammatical historical interpretation of the OT itself. The other comes from a grammatical historical analysis of the NT passage that cites it. The authority for the second meaning of the OT passage is not the OT; it is the NT. The OT produces only the literal meaning. The *sensus plenior* meaning emerges only after an ISPA of the OT wording to a new situation. The NT writers could assign such new meanings authoritatively because of the inspiration of what they wrote.[113]

Essentially, the NT writers are allowed to use the canonical or complementary hermeneutic by virtue of the inspiration of their words. While Thomas flatly denies that contemporary interpreters may legitimately engage in the same assignment of meaning, he does not offer any reason beyond the fact that "NT writers were directly inspired by God...current interpreters are not."[114]

Admittedly, Thomas' entire argument is well crafted, and plausibly legitimate in its conclusions. Hence, my complaint against the ISPA device might be petty, but it seems, for two

---

[112] Ibid.: 80.
[113] Ibid.: 80.
[114] Ibid.: 80.

reasons, a substantial problem that a nonliteral hermeneutic is advocated in Scripture. First, a nonliteral hermeneutic does violate the principle of single meaning, in that it adds a secondary meaning. Thomas asks and answers,

> Did God know from the beginning that the OT passage had two meanings?" The answer is obviously yes. But until the NT citation of that passage, the second or *sensus plenior* meaning did not exist as far as humans were concerned. Since hermeneutics is a human discipline, gleaning that second sense is an impossibility in an examination of the OT source of the citation. The additional meaning is therefore not a grammatical historical interpretation of the OT passage. The additional meaning is the fruit of grammatical historical interpretation of the companion NT passage. The OT passage has only a single meaning.[115]

Thomas admits divine use of double meaning, but, of course, God has that prerogative. This is not an entirely untenable position, but the question remains regarding whether or not this is a device God has chosen to employ in Scripture.

David Cooper represents a different explanation of seemingly nonliteral NT usage of OT passages. He appeals to what he calls the Law of Double Reference, which is "the principle of associating similar or related ideas which are usually separated from one another by long period of times, and which are blended into a single picture like the blending of

---

[115] Ibid.: 80.

pictures by a stereopticon."¹¹⁶ Arnold Fruchtenbaum offers a concise suggestion that the rule "observes the fact that often a passage or a block of Scripture is speaking of two different persons or two different events that are separated by a long period of time."¹¹⁷ Fruchtenbaum is careful to distinguish the axiom from double fulfillment, which anticipates more than one fulfillment of a particular prophecy.

Cooper sees LDR exemplified in Psalm 16:8-11. He suggests that each of the affirmations there represent experiences David did not personally have, though he uses the first person pronouns throughout. Cooper's argument is that the perceived tension between the pronouns and the experiences is no tension at all, but rather represents David's knowing and prophetic references to Messiah. His entire argument is worthy of representation here:

> But when we look at verses 8-11, we see that he still uses the personal pronouns (I, me, my, and mine) of the first person. At the same time we know that David did not enjoy the experiences that are mentioned here. To show that David was not speaking of his own experiences, I will quote these last four verses.
>
> 8 I have set Jehovah always before me: Because he is at my right hand, I shall not be moved. 9 Therefore my heart is glad, and my glory rejoiceth: My flesh also shall dwell

---

[116] David L. Cooper and Burl Haynie, "The Fifth Law: The Law of Double Reference" in *Rules of Interpretation: Articles from Biblical Research Monthly, 1947. 1949.* (Biblical Research Sosicety) at http://www.Biblicalresearch.info/page49.html.
[117] Arnold Fruchtenbaum, *Footsteps of the Messiah* (Ariel Ministries, 2003), 4-5.

in safety. 10 For thou wilt not leave my soul to Sheol; Neither wilt thou suffer thy holy one to see corruption. 11 Thou wilt show me the path of life: In thy presence is fullness of Joy; In thy right hand there are pleasures for evermore (Ps. 16:8-11).

The historic David did not keep the Lord always before him. He got his eyes off the Lord and fell, sinning most miserably and wretchedly. One unconfessed sin called for another, and that one, still unconfessed, called for another. David was enmeshed in a series of moral lapses and sins. He certainly was moved. His heart was not always glad. Neither did his soul rejoice; and his flesh was not always dwelling in safety. Moreover, when he died, he went to Sheol and, so far as the record goes, remained there. His body was placed in the tomb and saw corruption—that is, decomposition and decay. When he went down into Sheol, the Lord did not point out to him the path of life and he did not come forth.[118]

Cooper's LDR and the accompanying argument from Psalm 16 for its legitimacy offers the advantage of affirming a literal NT rendering of the OT passage. However, such a conclusion necessarily abandons single meaning in the OT passage. That seems not a particularly favorable trade.

Instead of such a profound hermeneutic maneuver, it seems more likely that the Psalmist was referring in verse 8 to his own positional relationship with his Lord – much like God called David a man after God's own heart (1 Sam 13:14). If LDR

---

[118] Cooper and Haynie, http://www.Biblicalresearch.info/page57.html.

is in view in verse 8, who is being referenced? Who is the "I" in verse 8? Did the Messiah have the Father at His right hand? That would create a directional contradiction with Ephesians 1:20, for example (Father and Son aren't both at each other's right hand are they?). Also, is there some concern on the Father's part about His being shaken? This is odd language if referring to God.

Further, verse 9 echoes an oft-repeated refrain from David that his relationship with the Lord brought him constant peace and joy. The references to that end are too numerous to list here. Should we assume that in all such cases LDR is in view?

If, on the other hand, David is actually referring in Psalm 16:8 to the Messiah as Yahweh,[119] then Peter's reference that "David says of Him…" would not require that Jesus fit *every* characteristic mentioned in the Psalm 16 quote, or that Jesus be the antecedent to the first person pronouns in the section. All that would be required for a literal rendering is that Jesus is the Lord (in Ps 16:8 and Acts 2:25), and that based on Acts 2:31, He was the "Holy One" who would not undergo decay (based on the resurrection theme of Peter's Acts 2:24-29).

There is no inherent exegetical reason to conclude that the first phrase of Psalm 16:10 and Acts 2:27 *needs* to refer to the same person as the second phrase of 16:10 and 2:27. In short, there is no reason to assume that the first person references to David should be applied to anyone other than him, because the third person references offer enough to support Peter's Acts 2:31 assertion that David anticipated the Messiah's resurrection.

---

[119] It is common in the OT for the pre-incarnate Messiah to be referred to by the name Yahweh, see e.g., Gen 12:1-7.

Even in Peter's apparent connection of "You will not abandon my soul to Hades" (Acts 2:27) with "He was not abandoned to Hades..." (2:31), Peter cites τὴν ψυχήν μου (first person singular) in the first phrase, while referencing simply the (aorist passive indicative, third person) verb ἐγκατελείφθη. First, Peter references the soul, then simply the person. Is it more probable that Peter is connecting the two because of a double reference in the whole passage, or that Peter is saying both are true of Jesus, even if David may have only intended the second phrase (with the third person) directly in reference to Jesus?

Both ISPA and LDR are plausible explanatory devices. Both have advantages, and it is possible that either is correct. However, both seem to possess significant disadvantages – specifically in that they fail to escape inconsistency on the pivotal issue of single meaning. It is due to that inconsistency that it seems worthwhile to seek a different model that might better represent the Author's intention for our understanding of the Text.

An Alternative Understanding of New Testament Use of the Old Testament: John's Parallelism of Foreshadowing and Fulfillment

ISPA allows for human authors to add divinely inspired secondary NT meanings to OT texts. LDR allows for God to have embedded secondary NT meanings within OT texts. If instead of working from the premises of these two allowances we worked from the premise that God and the human authors He employed all consistently utilized single meaning (as a necessary linguistic device), then what would be the best understanding of NT use of the OT? Such an understanding would need not only to alleviate the necessity for secondary meaning either in OT and NT, but would have to also hold up under exegetical scrutiny. John's parallelism of foreshadowing and fulfillment introduces us to such a model.

Johannine Use of πληρόω as Hermeneutic Indicator

John uses the lemma πληρόω fifteen times. Seven of those instances do not connect OT and NT passages (3:29, 7:8, 12:3, 15:11, 16:6, 16:24, 17:13), but rather speak of filling in the most literal sense (filling a room, joy being fulfilled, etc.). Another two instances of πληρόω reference the words of Christ, directly:

> ...to fulfill the word which He spoke, "Of those whom You have given Me I lost (aorist) not one" (18:9).

> to fulfill the word of Jesus which He spoke (aorist), signifying (present active participle) by what kind of death He was about to die (present active infinitive) (18:32).

The first of these refers back to John 17:12, but doesn't quote or reference the OT directly. It does, however give us indication that fulfillment is not necessarily connected to prediction. The second of these occurrences does refer to the occurrence of a predicted event. This shows that John's usage of fulfillment is nuanced, with at least two possible modes of operation: fulfillment related to direct prediction, and fulfillment unrelated to direct prediction.

Four occurrences of πληρόω are accompanied by aorist verbs translated directly from OT passages:

This was to fulfill the word of Isaiah the prophet which he spoke: "Lord, who has believed (aorist) our report? And to whom has the arm of the Lord been revealed (aorist)?" (12:38).

"I do not speak of all of you. I know the ones I have chosen; but it is that the Scripture may be fulfilled, 'He who eats My bread has lifted up (aorist) his heel against Me' (13:18).

"But they have done this to fulfill the word that is written in their Law, 'They hated (aorist) Me without a cause.' (15:25).

So they said to one another, "Let us not tear it, but cast lots for it, to decide whose it shall be"; this was to fulfill the Scripture: "They divided (aorist) My outer garments among them, and for My clothing they cast lots (aorist)." Therefore the soldiers did these things (19:24-25).

In the latter three instances (13:18, 15:25, 19:24), the OT referents are not overtly predictive, but refer to recorded experiences of David in Psalm 41:9, 35:15, 69:4, 22:18, respectively. It is entirely possible that David wrote these Psalms as predictive, but there is no internal indication that he did, and they match (even if only poetically) his own personal experience. The implication is that these are later applied to Jesus, not because of their predictive nature, *but because in some way they were foreshadowing – or prior illustrations – of something that would later take place.*

The first reference, from Isaiah 53, does seem predictive in the sense that the entire chapter discusses the incarnation and death of Messiah. There was no historical referent during Isaiah's time that fit the chapter 53 description. So in this instance, fulfillment seems to indicate the happening of a directly predicted event.

Two of the remaining four occurrences of πληρόω make allusion to the OT without quoting it:

> While I was with them, I was keeping them in Your name which You have given Me; and I guarded them and not one of them perished (aorist) but the son of perdition, so that the Scripture would be fulfilled (17:12).

Here Jesus alludes to Psalm 41:9, though he doesn't quote the passage (of course, His Father knew the passage). The passage referenced is not predictive, but lacks fulfillment or completion until it is embodied in the ministry of Christ.

There is still yet another reference from John that helps us to understand John's foreshadowing and fulfillment model. This one is particularly helpful because it helps the reader to understand that John is using *fulfillment* and *completion* as virtually synonymous concepts:

> After this, Jesus, knowing that all things had already been accomplished, to fulfill the Scripture, said, "I am thirsty" (19:28).

Here John connects the idea of fulfillment with accomplishment or completion. In this instance John uses τελειωθῇ rather than πληρόω to indicate completion of, presumably, Psalm 69:21. This is a Psalm of David, and throughout the Psalm, the Lord is referred to in the second person, and David is in the first person. There is nothing in the Psalm that demands the first person be divine. John's use of τελειωθῇ here helps us understand that Psalm 69:21 was not predictive, but rather a foreshadowing of a later event. John does not redact the meaning of the Psalm (from Davidic first person to divine first person). Rather it seems he is assigning *purpose* to the OT writing: the events of Psalm 69:21 were incomplete (in need of fulfillment) until a very similar – or nearly identical – event happened to Jesus.

John's use of πληρόω and τελειωθῇ gives us insight into his view of fulfillment not as necessarily and always the occurrence of a predicted event. Instead, John seems to recognize OT referents often as foreshadowing, or illustrations beforehand, which point to the coming Messiah. It is much like the concept made evident in the prescription of Exodus 12:46. The Passover Lamb was to have no broken bones. There was no prediction accompanying the prescription. Nonetheless, regardless of whether or not the initial recipients of that prescription understood the symbol of the unbroken bones (as foreshadowing of the coming Messiah, who would be the ultimate Passover Lamb with unbroken bones), they were given a prescription that would remind them of their deliverance. The primary application of the prescription was clear, and they were to obey it literally. LGH in the OT, and then LGH in the NT – there is no evolution in the hermeneutic model employed from Moses to John. That John is advocating the concept of foreshadowing and fulfillment is even more evident by his use of the term σημεῖον.

John's Use of σημεῖον as Hermeneutic Indicator

John uses the lemma σημεῖον seventeen times in his Gospel. In eight of those instances John uses them as narrative markers. In the first of those mentions, John describes Jesus' signs as manifestations of His glory, and as having the outcome of the disciples' belief in Him:

> This beginning of *His* signs Jesus did in Cana of Galilee, and manifested His glory, and His disciples believed in Him (2:11).

In the second of John's seven narrative markers, he again connects Jesus' signs with the outcome of belief:

> Now when He was in Jerusalem at the Passover, during the feast, many believed in His name, observing His signs which He was doing (2:23).

The third reference minimally descriptive, though it introduces a numerical continuation from the first mention:

> This is again a second sign that Jesus performed when He had come out of Judea into Galilee (4:54).

The fourth and sixth references both describe the outcome of His signs not as belief, but as a following. The fifth occurrence carries with it the recognition on the part of some who acknowledged the Messiah had come:

> A large crowd followed Him, because they saw the signs which He was performing on those who were sick (6:2).

> Therefore when the people saw the sign which He had performed, they said, "This is truly the Prophet who is to come into the world" (6:14).

> For this reason also the people went and met Him, because they heard that He had performed this sign (12:18).

The penultimate of these mentions describes the outcome of unbelief. The progression was complete. At the first performance of the signs, there was belief, then mere following, and finally, unbelief:

> But though He had performed so many signs before them, *yet* they were not believing in Him (12:37).

The final narrative marker using σημεῖον includes John's purpose statement, that the signs were recorded so that the reader would believe in Him and have life in His name:

> Therefore many other signs Jesus also performed in the presence of the disciples, which are not written in this book; but these have been written so that you may believe that Jesus is the Christ, the Son of God; and that believing you may have life in His name (20:30-31).

The purpose and progression evident here in John's Gospel is significant. Signs are employed not as ends in themselves, but as purposed for belief. The narrative journey undertaken by John in his Gospel culminates in the wrong response by those who witnessed the signs, and ultimately calls readers to a positive response to the evidence presented through the signs. Even though the signs were actual happenings that are communicated via single meaning, they were illustrative – manifestations – of the glory of the Messiah. This is a vital principle in the JPFF model for understanding NT use of the OT: *there was no metaphor involved in the communication of these events, yet the events themselves were metaphor designed to invoke a response.*

In seven more occurrences of σημεῖον John uses the term quoting people who are either responding verbally to Jesus, or talking about Him to others. The first and third of these instances shows that signs were associated with evidence of Messianic identity. The Jews had a Scriptural expectation that the Messiah would come with signs to demonstrate who He was. Similarly, the second instance expands on the concept of Messianic authentication and identification. The expected signs would come through divine empowerment:

> The Jews then said to Him, "What sign do You show us as your authority for doing these things?" (2:18).

> this man came to Jesus by night and said to Him, "Rabbi, we know that You have come from God *as* a teacher; for no one can do these signs that You do unless God is with him" (3:2).

> So they said to Him, "What then do You do for a sign, so that we may see, and believe You? What work do You perform?" (6:30).

Jesus' signs were so significant, and so parallel to what was expected of Messiah, that the fourth instance in this category underscores a broad public understanding that Jesus was indeed meeting the authentication and identification expectations with respect to signs performed. Any unbelief there might have been was no result of a failure on His part to fulfill Scriptural expectations:

> But many of the crowd believed in Him; and they were saying, "When the Christ comes, He will not perform more signs than those which this man has, will He?" (7:31).

Still, there was confusion on the part of many leaders. Their expectations had gone beyond what was revealed in the Text. Their understanding of the Sabbath exceeded the Biblical mandate. Because of that faulty evaluation, they mischaracterized Him as a sinner. Thus their legalism blinded them to the identity of their Messiah, as evidenced by the fifth mention of σημεῖον in this context:

> Therefore some of the Pharisees were saying, "This man is not from God, because He does not keep the Sabbath." But others were saying, "How can a man who is a sinner perform such signs?" And there was a division among them (9:16).

Though John's message was not authenticated by signs of his own, he fulfilled his ministry of preparing the way for and announcing the Messiah. In this sixth reference, many recognized that the signs of Jesus' ministry not only showed the authenticity of Jesus' ministry, but John's as well:

> Many came to Him and were saying, "While John performed no sign, yet everything John said about this man was true" (10:41).

Tragically, in the final of the references in this category, the leaders are now concerned with how they can stop Jesus, because the evidence of His signs is so great, and many are believing in Him. These leaders are in fear for the future of a system that was a fiction and not Biblically derived, yet their loyalties to the system did not allow them to see their own grave error:

> Therefore the chief priests and the Pharisees convened a council, and were saying, "What are we doing? For this man is performing many signs (11:47).

In the two remaining instances of σημεῖον in John's Gospel, Jesus is speaking, first in response to the royal official whose son was sick. He challenges the people listening (referring to the second person plural, not directly only to the royal official), that they would require evidence for the claims being made:

> So Jesus said to him, "Unless you *people* see signs and wonders, you *simply* will not believe" (4:48).

After making the statement, the official demonstrated his faith by insisting Jesus come to heal His son. Jesus rewarded His faith with the miraculous healing of his son – a miracle that demonstrated Jesus' Messianic identity.

In the final occurrence in this category, Jesus reminds the crowd that their interest in Him extended beyond the performing of signs to their own realization of personal benefit. He calls them to belief in Him, claiming ultimately to be the bread from heaven:

> Jesus answered them and said, "Truly, truly, I say to you, you seek Me, not because you saw signs, but because you ate of the loaves and were filled (6:26).

The signs recorded in John's Gospel served the specific purpose as demonstrative of the Messiah's divinity and identity. Those who witnessed His signs understood much of the Messianic expectation set by Scripture, and Jesus Himself recognized that the works He did provided resounding testimony to His claim as Messiah (Jn 5:36). The signs demonstrate a precedent – both in revelation and expectation – that the Messiah would fulfill Scripture *literally*, and in so doing prove His identity. The problem was that the people expected literal fulfillment of the miraculous signs. They got what they expected in that regard, but some failed to expect literal fulfillment of Messianic suffering and sacrificial death (as in Isaiah 53). In that, they got what they didn't expect, and as had been predicted, many stumbled over Him, fulfilling literally that prediction.[120]

John's use of σημεῖον and his connection by that term of Scriptural, Messianic expectation and fulfillment illustrate that

---

[120] Is 8:14, Mt 16:19, 1 Pet 2:4-10.

John recognized a kind of parallelism between the miracles, or signs, and the truth to which they pointed. That truth was embodied in the Christ. *He* is the antecedent that the events were designed to unveil. The miracles were events that literally happened and were communicated literally, but they were illustrative of something much greater: *Him*. And it is with this concept of the *parallelism of foreshadowing and fulfillment* in mind that we can understand John's use of the OT in a fulfillment context.

Sometimes John identifies fulfillment as a happening of a predicted event. Sometimes he presents fulfillment as the culmination of a foreshadowing. Sometimes that foreshadowing is specifically quoted from the OT, other times it is more general and not tied to a particular passage. But in every Johannine fulfillment context, there is no hermeneutic adjustment of OT meaning for the NT usage, nor is there any hint of a shift from plain and single meaning.

Conclusion: The JPFF Model Considered for Broader Application

John's parallelism of foreshadowing and fulfillment provides a model whereby we can understand that the OT was written with single meaning in view, that the NT does not adjust or alter that meaning, and that Biblical meaning is not subject to change in any context. John's hermeneutic approach to the foreshadowing of the Messiah and fulfillment of that foreshadowing in Christ through His signs and other activities provides a significant hermeneutic precedent for Biblical interlocutors of today. The parallelism in John's writing between the metaphorical anticipation and the literal realization goes far beyond the simple predication and coming to pass of events.

In Matthew 16:4 and Luke 11:29 Jesus identified Jonah as a sign pointing to Himself. Notably, both writers use the same terminology (σημεῖον) employed by John. Jonah's water adventures literally happened, and they were communicated in a narrative way that demands normative, literal understanding. Yet, Jesus presented those events as a sign pointing to Himself – specifically to His burial and resurrection. The events of Jonah were not in themselves metaphorical, nor were they communicated with any anticipation of metaphorical interpretation, yet Jesus utilized those events as a metaphor that was fulfilled – or culminated –in Him.

Just as a pronoun has an antecedent, foreshadowing has fulfillment. In grammatical analogy, the fulfillment is the antecedent and the foreshadowing is the pronoun. The pronoun has single meaning and only one referent, but the *usage* may not be fully understood by the reader until the antecedent is identified in the text. Rather than appeal to ISPA or LDR to understand the connection between Psalm 16 and Acts 2, for example, we could apply the JPFF model and understand that Psalm 16 was referencing David's personal experience when he used the first person, the Father when he used the second person, and the Son when he used the third person. We are not informed that David looked forward to the resurrection until Peter tells us so (Acts 2:31), so when we read the passage without Peter's enlightenment, we are not bereft of any of its *meaning*, we just don't know of the passage's full *usage*. In the same way, we don't know simply from a reading of Jonah how those historical events will be *used* later in God's plan.

In short, where ISPA and LDR are wrestling with the potential of changing meanings, JPFF argues for a set and unchanged meaning with augmented *usage*. This is the great advantage of JPFF over ISPA and LDR. Change in meaning is the subject matter of hermeneutic significance. Change in usage has nothing whatsoever to do with hermeneutics, but is more a question of aesthetics. God's ultimate purpose to glorify Himself and demonstrate His own character is an *aesthetic* enterprise, and His *use* of literal happenings as metaphor contributes greatly to that enterprise. JPFF invites us to resolve the issue of whether there is change in meaning and consider the aesthetic function of OT passages referenced in the NT.

Appendix: Comparing JPFF with Three Non-Classical Dispensational Models

Perhaps in hopes of arriving at a better alternative to ISPA and LDR, Walter Kaiser, Darrell Bock, and Peter Enns advocate for three different views on NT use of the OT. Kaiser proposes a view suggesting there is single meaning and unified referents, Bock recognizes single meaning with multiple referents and contexts, and Enns argues for a fuller meaning with but a single goal.[121]

Kaiser recognizes "wide acceptance of *sensus plenior* among contemporary evangelicals,"[122] and suggests this acceptance as underscoring the need for the conversation. Kaiser concedes that the "deeper meaning of *sensus plenior* cannot be found in an exegesis of the OT text."[123] Further, he defines eisegesis in this context as, "reading backwards from the NT into the OT texts new meanings not discoverable by the rules of

---

[121] Gundry, Berding, and Lunde, general editors, *Three Views on the New Testament Use of the Old Testament*, (Grand Rapids, MI: Zondervan, 2008) Kindle Version, Location 521.
[122] Location 876.
[123] Location 942.

language and exegesis."[124] He borrows E.D Hirsch's distinction between meaning (which is unchanging) and significance (which can vary per context), and illustrates change in significance by quoting S. Lewis Johnson on Psalm 41:10 as alluded to in John 13:8 – "The logic...found here is...simply this...David prefigured the Messiah...Jesus' use of an Old Testament type may have been the pedagogical precursor for Peter's similar use of the Psalms in Acts 1:16."[125] Kaiser concludes "One need only to distinguish meaning from significance as E. D. Hirsch has argued all along,"[126] and consequently, "all Scripture is inspired by God and remains useful – not always for the same thing, but in no way is it declared to be antiquated and subject to new meanings from subsequent Biblical writers or readers."[127]

Bock builds his own argument on the premise that, while the OT context plays a significant role in how a passage us used, it is not the only factor.[128] Bock's key premise is, "that God works both in his words *and* in revelatory events that also help to elaborate his message...the use of the OT in the NT is not just about texts; it is about God's revelatory acts. The two often combine in prediction and pattern, to show what God is doing in history through word and deed."[129] Bock's approach seems nearly to blur the special revelation / natural revelation distinction, regarding God's actions as communication. Thus God's revelation is not merely God-breathed, but also God-accomplished (my term). Further, Bock lists as the fifth of six theological presuppositions in understanding the NT use of the

---

[124] Ibid.
[125] Location 1136-1149.
[126] Location 1527.
[127] Location 1566.
[128] Location 1988.
[129] Ibid.

OT "Now and not yet (the inaugurated fulfillment of Scripture),"[130] and includes it as one of the "crucial underpinnings of how to read the OT..."[131] This is an example of a theological hermeneutic, and on these points shows marked difference from JPFF. JPFF shares the same advantages over Bock's view as it does over ISPA – where Bock is trying to come to grips with apparent change in meaning, JPFF acknowledges only change in usage. With respect to meaning, JPFF possesses a greater degree of objectivity over Bock's single meaning, multiple referents/contexts view.

Enns offers a view rooted in the question of how true it is that hermeneutic tensions are actually at odds with an inspired text.[132] Enns suggests his effort is "to recognize that God is the God of history, and Scripture is God's gracious revelation of himself and his actions in the concrete, everyday world of ancient Semitic and Hellenistic peoples..."[133] Enns argues that the "NT authors' engagement of their Scripture was not directed by grammatical historical principles."[134] Instead, he views Second Temple literary practices and traditions as of "self evident" value in understanding the NT use of the OT.[135] Enns doesn't view the Scriptures as exegetically different than Second Temple literature. Instead, the major difference is thematic – the Scriptures are Christotelic, whereas other literature isn't. Hence, the distinctive is not derived hermeneutically, but rather thematically.[136] Consequently, Paul's (for example) hermeneutic

---

[130] Location 2053.
[131] Ibid.
[132] Location 3135.
[133] Location 3148.
[134] Location 3196.
[135] Location 3206, 3221.
[136] Location 3260.

model is determined by his times, and we should seek to follow the apostolic model – which means to understand what Paul was doing before we can understand what the text means to us today.[137]

In Enns' view, OT meaning changes for NT writers, and meaning changes for us as well. Meaning is not a constant, though the thematic center (Christ) remains the same. "The interpretation of the OT by the NT authors is embedded in their cultural moment."[138] Because of this changing meaning, Enns refers to Scripture as being humiliated, much like Christ was humiliated.[139] Ultimately, Enns' "Christotelic approach" is a reframing of a redemptive hermeneutic, and is, like Bock's, a theological hermeneutic above all. It is worth noting that Enns does not view his hermeneutic as a method that can be learned as if from a manual. He suggest "God's word is too rich, deep, and subtle for that. But following the NT authors – or better, committing ourselves to learning more and more just what that means – is indispensable for Christian interpretation of the OT.[140] Enns' view is markedly distinct form JPFF. Meaning changes, and is driven thematically based on a theological presupposition.

Of these three views, Kaiser's seems very close to JPFF, recognizing the distinction between meaning and usage, and preferring to understand that meaning does not change, though usage does.

---

[137] Location 3379.
[138] Location 3669.
[139] Location 3693.
[140] Location 3923.

9

PRIORITY OF HERMENEUTICS IN RESOLVING TEXTUAL DIFFICULTIES:
THE HEBREWS' WARNING PASSAGES[141]

The Letter to the Hebrews is theologically rich, and is both informative and practical. The writer of the letter explains the superiority of Christ and our need to respond to Him properly, and warns readers in eight passages of the consequences for failing to walk properly with Christ (2:1-3, 3:12-13, 4:1-11, 6:1-8, and 10:19-31, 12:14-17, 12:25-29, and 13:4-6). But are these warnings related to the position, practice, or destiny of believers – or all of the above? Considering these passages together in context helps us think through what God expects of us and what we should expect of Him.

The Central Issues

The so-called warning passages of Hebrews have been understood historically in a number of ways, four of which are considered here: (1) the evangelistic view – as warning unbelievers of positional consequences of unbelief, specifically eternal condemnation, (2) the loss of salvation view – as warning believers of positional consequences of post-salvation sin,

---

[141] Originally presented as "Grace in the Hebrews' Warning Passages: Why They Matter and What They Say," to the Free Grace Alliance National Conference, Arlington, Texas, October 11, 2016.

namely loss of salvation, (3) the loss of status view – as warning believers of practical consequences of post-salvation sin, specifically loss of access to certain benefits in the kingdom and eternity, and (4) the loss of progress view – as warning believers of practical consequences of post-salvation sin, specifically loss of progress in their growth.

The differences between these views are very significant for at least two important reasons. First, the hermeneutic and theological methods used to derive the conclusions are different. To prefer one conclusion over another requires preferring one interpretive strategy over another. In my estimation this is the most significant issue at stake, because the interpretive approach will go a long way in determining how one understands Scripture, and ultimately the character and work of God. Second, the conclusions drawn regarding the warning passages of Hebrews impact fundamental aspects of salvation – namely justification, sanctification, and glorification.

Methodology and Hermeneutic Implications

How should we approach passages that present apparent challenges to central tenets? The simple answer is we should handle them the same way as we would handle any passage of Scripture. Adjusting methodology to make Scripture more palatable has historically had abysmal results. For example, the Alexandrian theologian Philo modeled this reparative[142] approach by allegorizing much of the Hebrew Bible to make it, well, less Hebrew, and to help it correspond more with Greek thought. Philo understood Genesis 2:10-15 as not referring to

---

[142] I mean reparative in the sense that the motivation was to repair the text and resolve or remove perceived problems.

four literal rivers, but rather as representative of four virtues.[143] Philo viewed the Genesis creation accounts more as moral metaphor than as literal history. The motivation of redeeming or repairing the text from uncomfortable literalities moved Philo to usher in a longstanding era of reader-centric interpretation that did not waver until the Reformation, and has since come back into vogue. In Philo's approach the reader is at the center, and the author's communicated meaning is no longer the central issue. In this approach, the ultimate authority over the text's meaning is not the author, but the reader.

Imagine an artist who paints a beautiful seascape, using a great variety of shades and colors, with articulate detail. As the artist proudly presents the painting to the public, he offers a narrative of the meaning and significance of the painting. One aficionado attending the presentation raises his hand and begins to correct the artist, suggesting that the artist is mistaken – the painting is not a seascape at all. Clearly, it is simply a metaphor of the psychological struggles of the post-modern, post-colonial, south-central, middle-class, disenfranchised, not-yet-unionized, millennial, gluten free, retail workers community.

A child standing nearby peers at the painting with squinting eyes, then looks at the dissenting interpreter, then back at the painting, then back at the interpreter. And she doesn't say what she is thinking, though it is written all over her face: "Are adults really this dissociative (because all children use the word dissociative)? Clearly this is a painting of wind-driven water and a distant coastland." Further, the little girl intuitively

---

[143] Philo, "Allegorical Interpretation of Genesis 2,3", in *The Works of Philo* (Loeb Classical Library), 142-143, viewed at https://www.loebclassics.com/view/philo_judaeus-allegorical_interpretation_genesis_i_ii/1929/pb_LCL226.143.xml.

knows that the painter gets to determine meaning, not the pompous art interlocutor (because, of course, all children use the word interlocutor, too). What that girl intuitively understands is sometimes lost on us. If we recognize divine authorship of Scripture (as I do), then we must understand that the Author of Scripture communicated meaning, He intends to be understood, and He used human languages to communicate. Our job as readers is to understand what He has communicated, not to attribute meaning.

One particular interpretive device often employed in understanding of challenging passages like the warning passages of Hebrews is called the *analogy of faith*. In the analogy of faith, the reader compares a difficult passage with other related passages that might be easier to understand. The reader concludes that the difficult passage must essentially agree with the simpler ones. While there is merit to this approach, as we would certainly expect Scripture to agree with Scripture, the danger inherent in the approach is to think topically rather than contextually. Each passage, in its own context, stands alone, with respect to communicating meaning. It is important to look at broader contexts and even topically related passages, but if our understanding of those other passages is flawed in any way, it creates a domino effect, as we reproduce our misunderstanding with each passage we consider through the lens of analogy of faith. If we are not careful, we bring too much preunderstanding to the study of a passage. So our approach should be, first and foremost, concerned with the immediate context of any passage.

For example, you might conclude as I do that when we consider collectively passages like John 14:1-3, 1 Corinthians 15:50-58, 1 Thessalonians 4:13-17, and 2 Thessalonians 2:1-10, that the Bible plainly teaches a return of Christ to the atmosphere of earth to resurrect believers who have died and to remove believers who are alive at that time, prior to the beginning of Daniel's seventieth week. So, having that theological understanding, when we read Matthew 24:31[144] we might think topically and read our rapture understanding into that passage. In doing so, we would completely miss the immediate context's clear indications that Matthew 24:31 has nothing whatsoever to do with the event we call the rapture. Yet there are enough thematic points of similarity between the rapture passages and Matthew 24:31 that we might incorrectly infer thematic sameness.

Another interpretive device that can come into play in considering Hebrews is what we might call *metaphor matching*. It is an approach to understanding figures, illustrations, and parable by trying to find a one-for-one match of the metaphorical components in the reality that is being illustrated. Metaphor matching stretches the limits of metaphor, trying to find comprehensive correspondence beyond what might have been intended by the author. Just as the Gospels record many parables intended to communicate kingdom characteristics, Hebrews employs many Old Testament citations to illustrate truths pertaining to church age believers. In both contexts we need to be careful not to understand the illustrations as the primary vehicle for didactic content. They aren't the point. They are, however, intended to help us understand the point.

To put it plainly here is the caution I offer: as we seek to understand the meaning of any passage, we need to follow the

---

[144] "And He will send forth His angels with a great trumpet and they will gather together His elect from the four winds, from one end of the sky to the other."

normative, literal grammatical historical rules for understanding written communication. We need to avoid reading any theological pre-commitments into any passage, even if metaphor provides ample opportunity to insert those pre-commitments. In short, I cannot bring a free-grace position to any passage. I must submit to the text in its context, allowing God to say what He has said, and I must adjust my theology to fit what the text says.

For the purpose of this present discussion, as we approach the warning passages in Hebrews, we must not read them as dispensational thinkers or as reformed thinkers, nor as free grace, ultra-free grace,[145] or lordship thinkers. We must read them as submissive learners, ready to listen to what God has communicated, and ready to change our minds accordingly.

Justification, Sanctification, and Glorification Implications

It is evident that in the New Testament salvation from sin has three basic applications: (1) the positional aspect, otherwise known as justification, (2) the progressive or practical aspect, otherwise known as sanctification, and (3) the ultimate or eschatological aspect, otherwise known as glorification. If in any mention of salvation we do not parse correctly which of the three is in view, we will likely have a flawed view of all three. In the four interpretive perspectives on the warning passages considered here, there is understood an emphasis on motivating

---

[145] Ultra-free grace is a term I use frequently to describe Zane Hodges' and GES' view of grace, to distinguish it from the view espoused by Chafer and Ryrie for example. I intend the term not as pejorative, but as descriptive. While both groups have appealed to the term free grace, the distinctions between the two are monumental, and significant enough to warrant a transparent distinction in nomenclature.

to action. The distinctions evident between the four views are most obvious in comparing the bases for the action.

The first (evangelistic) view understands the calls to action as motivating change to positional salvation. The second (loss of salvation) view understands the calls to action as motivation to practical or progressive salvation by threatening the loss of positional salvation. The third (loss of status) view understands the calls to action as motivation to practical or progressive salvation by threatening loss in ultimate or eschatological salvation, and thereby changing the believer's final destiny.[146] The fourth (loss of progress) view understands the calls to action as motivation to practical or progressive salvation by focusing on what has already been accomplished in position and what is assured eschatologically. In a general sense, two views motivate to action by denying or questioning positional salvation. Another motivates to action by questioning eschatological or ultimate salvation. A more balanced approach (in this writer's estimation) motivates to action not by questioning either the positional or eschatological, but by appealing to both.

---

[146] Toussaint, for example, suggests a variation of this third view: "In all five warning passages of Hebrews the thing to be avoided by the original readers of that discourse was not loss of believers' rewards but loss of salvation. Quite clearly the writer knew of a group in that early congregation who had made professions of faith in Jesus Christ but were in peril of jettisoning their confessions to apostatize and lapse back into Judaism. The prophetic elements in the warnings confirm this interpretation." Toussaint arrives at this conclusion by viewing the salvation to be lost not as positional but eschatological (Stanley Toussaint, "The Eschatology of the Warning Passages in Hebrews" in *Grace Theological Journal* 3.1 (Spring, 1982): 80.).

Introduction to Hebrews
Authorship

We don't know the identity of the author of Hebrews, though we can discern from 2:2-3 that it was not an apostle. The author speaks of the gospel as being spoken through the Lord and confirmed through signs miracles, wonders, and gifts to us by those who heard. Though not an apostle, it is likely that the author worked closely with one or more of the apostles, and with Timothy (13:23). It is also evident that the writer possessed a thorough knowledge of the Old Testament, as the epistle makes frequent reference to and application of the Old Testament.

Audience

The identity of the initial audience is a very important factor in understanding the calls to action in Hebrews. There are viable arguments that Hebrews was written to a mixed audience of believers and unbelievers, but this commentator suggests that the nine references to the audience as brethren,[147] including one as holy brethren, along with the call that the readers should not lay again a foundation of faith in God (6:1) – these are suggestive that the writer is talking to believers. Of course, if this view is correct, then the perspective that Hebrews is evangelistic, and that the warning passages are for the exhortation of unbelievers is not tenable. However, this study of the warning passages will not presuppose the salvation of the audience, but will try to determine that key component from those particular contexts.

---

[147] 2:11, 2:12, 2:17, 3:1, 3:12, 7:5, 10:19, 13:1, 13:22.

Purpose

The writer identifies the writing as a word of exhortation, and urges readers to hold up under it (13:22), challenging them to maturity and endurance in light of the supremacy of Christ. That summative characterization of the writing as a word of exhortation is fitting, as the letter vacillates between two main literary devices. First, the author describes the supremacy of Jesus Christ, and then second, prescribes that the readers respond to Him. In those sections that include calls to action, some of the passages include warnings of negative consequences and some do not. Considering both the descriptions (of Christ as supreme) and the prescriptions (to respond properly to Him), readers have a clear picture of what is expected from them.

Structure
1-2 – Christ is Superior to Angels, Exhortation: Pay Attention
3 – Christ is Superior to Moses, Exhortation: Guard Your Hearts
4 – Exhortation: Fear, Draw Near with Confidence
5 – Christ is a Superior High Priest (Perfect)
6 – Exhortation: Press on to Maturity
7 – Christ is a Superior High Priest (Eternal)
8:1-10:18 – Christ is a Superior Mediator
10:19-39 – Exhortation: Don't Throw Away Confidence
11 – Examples of the Faith
12-13 – Exhortation: Walk with the Author and Perfecter of the Faith

Observing the Warning Passages

There are eight passages in the Epistle to the Hebrews that contain three signature elements: (1) a call to action, (2) a connective "for" or "so that," and (3) a statement of negative consequences if the call to action is not heeded. Because these three elements together constitute a warning for the reader, these are the passages counted here as warning passages: 2:1-3a, 3:12-14, 4:1-11, 6:1-8, 10:19-31, 12:14-17, 12:25-29, 13:4-6.

2:1-3a and 12:25-29

The call to action in 2:1-3a is based on the previous truths about the superiority of Jesus Christ, and the Father's speaking through Him: readers should hold more emphatically (*perissoteros prosechein*) to that which was spoken, in contrast to having a neglected salvation. If the reader doesn't heed this call, there are two implied negative consequences. Neither are explicit. First, by heeding the call to action, we might not alongside-drift (*pararuomen*). The second negative consequence is that we shall not escape (*ekpheuxometha*), but there is no direct indication of what it is that will not be escaped. The writer of Hebrews uses this term also in 12:25, with no specific mention of what is not being escaped. There are significant contextual parallels between 2:1-3 and 12:25-29 in this regard. The call to action in 12:25-29 is to not refuse (*paraitesthesthe*) the One speaking. This is similar to 2:1, which calls the reader to hold more emphatically to the word. Both passages are encouraging the reader to value that which had been spoken (about the Christ). Both question how one failing to heed can escape. Neither context specifies what will not be escaped, though it seems clear by contrast what will not be escaped. In 2:1 the escape seems to be from drifting away. If the word is held to, there will be escape from drifting away.

The escape in 12:25 is not any identified any more specifically than that of 2:1. The exhortation is to not refuse the one who is speaking. In the immediately preceding context (12:18-24) there is a reminder that Christ's blood was superior to the sprinkled blood of the Mosaic Covenant, and even to the blood of Abel, and that it is His blood that is speaking (12:24), and consequently, Jesus Himself is speaking. Israel refused God at Mt. Sinai and did not escape the promised consequences for disobedience (Ex 32), though God was merciful, and did not extend the judgment to the point He would have violated His word regarding Israel's future blessing. God demonstrated grace even in His judging of Israel. It is important to understand that God tempered His own wrath in light of His word (Deut 9:19-29). The writer of Hebrews warns readers not to refuse Christ as Israel had refused God.

These two warning passages are specific enough to dogmatically prefer one of the four interpretations over the others. That the author uses *we* (2:1, 2:3, 12:25, 12:28), and that the author adds that *we* are receiving an unshakeable or enduring kingdom (12:28), would seem to support an understanding that these passages are speaking only of believers, as believers have already been transferred to His kingdom (Col 1:13). Because we are receiving that kingdom, and because it is enduring, there is no change in what we are receiving. This concept would not support the idea that believers lose position or status in this kingdom. These warnings seem practical rather than positional or eschatological, and are rooted in the character of God and the present-tense walk of believers with Him.

3:12-14

After demonstrating the superiority of Christ over Moses as faithful over His house in comparison to Moses' faithfulness in his house, the writer warns readers to see to it that they do not have an unbelieving heart (3:12) to stand off (*apostenai*) from God. The outcome to be avoided is a heart hardened by the deceitfulness of sin (3:13). While there is no other specific consequence cited in this context, these verses bridge to the warning in 4:1-11, which names the negative consequence. Because this is a *supporting* warning passage, we move to the primary one in the broader context in search of specifics.

4:1-11

The calls to action are to fear (4:1) and to be diligent (4:11). The negative consequence in 4:1 of failing to fear is that one might think (*doke*) some of you might be lacking. Importantly, this passage does not say that if one does not fear, they don't enter the rest. The negative consequence of failing to be diligent in 4:11 is to fall (*pese*), in following the example of disobedience. Verses 2-10 help make clear what verses 1 and 11 are suggesting.

Verse 2 introduces a contrast between those who heard the good news and did not believe, and (we) who have heard the good news and have believed. Verse 3 adds that we are brought in (*eiserchometha*) who have believed (*pisteusantes*). The remainder of verse 3 through 6 describes why God has a rest, and why those who had previously disobeyed (namely a particular generation of Israelites) did not enter His rest. The writer references Psalm 95:7 and the limitations of Joshua's ministry (4:7-8) to help the reader understand that there remains a sabbath rest for the people of God (4:9). At this point it is important to recognize that when the writer of Hebrews refers to the people of God, Israel is in view.[148] The writer is not specifying that there remains a rest of God for the church, but rather for those who have not yet believed but one day will (specifically in this case, Israel). Those who have believed have already ceased from works, and instead rely on faith.

The verse 11 call to action is an aorist subjunctive, as is the conditional result, but the prescription is in the first person plural, while the conditional result is third person singular – we must be diligent (*spoudasomen*) so that one might not fall (*pese*). The same is true of the 4:1 call to action: *we must fear* is aorist subjunctive, first person plural (*phobethomen*), while *one might think* (*doke*) is an aorist subjunctive, third person singular. The implications of the grammatical distinction is significant: this is clearly not saying that if an individual is not diligent they will not enter His rest. This kind of construction seems similar to Philippians 2:12 – it is an exhortation to "work out your salvation with fear and trembling." That passage also does not warn of a consequence for an individual who fails, but motivates to action based on what has already been provided.

This context does not support the evangelistic understanding, as the *we* have already believed. It doesn't support the loss of salvation view, for even the consequence of *to fall* is not connected with a change in position. Further, this passage doesn't support the loss of status view, for there is no implication of what status might be lost, nor is there an implication that those who believe might end up with differing results. In fact, there is also no indication even of lost reward here. Instead, the message is simple: let us fear and be diligent,

---

[148] Note also 11:25, which contrasts the Israelites and the Egyptians.

otherwise one might think they have fallen short, or one might even fall into disobedience. This is a much more general exhortation than it is a specific warning, and it seems to pertain to the ongoing walk rather than a change in position or eschatological destiny.

6:1-8

The call to action is that we might move toward the completeness (*ten teleioteta pherometha*), having already moved beyond the beginning of the word of Christ (by having believed), and not laying down again a foundation that has already been laid (of repentance, faith, and basic information). Verses 4-6 contain what in English appears to be a progression of unrelated states of being and action, but the Greek grammatical structure really makes this section very simple.

Having been enlightened, having tasted, having become partakers, having tasted, and having fallen alongside, are all plural aorist participles. The ones these participles describe cannot be renewed to repentance while they are in this condition because they are (present tense) crucifying Christ again to themselves. Simply put, when persons are in the condition of having all five characteristics, they cannot change their mind (repent), otherwise they would no longer be in that state. So if they remain in that state, they are thus useless for pressing on to maturity. Thus the readers, who in this context are most certainly believers, are to press on to maturity, and avoid the state of being fallen alongside (*parapesontas*). The use of this term sends us back to 4:11, where the readers are cautioned against falling.

This context is clearly speaking of believers (they have repentance, faith in God, and have begun the process of sanctification), so the evangelistic view is not supported here. The loss of salvation view doesn't work with the grammatical construction. Grant Osborne, in support of the loss of salvation view (what he calls a classical Arminian view), suggests that "Hebrews is describing a very real danger of apostasy that true believers can commit, and if they do so it is an unpardonable sin from which there is no possibility of repentance, but only of eternal judgment."[149] He is correct with the first part – only true believers can meet the five conditions, but I believe he is wrong on the second part: there is no possibility of repentance *while being in the state of falling alongside*, so one would have to stop being fallen alongside, and then they could again resume their process of a changing mind and their journey toward completeness.

Neither the evangelistic view nor the loss of salvation view is supported here. The loss of status view is also not derivative from this text. It speaks not of the distant future – of life during the earthly coming of the kingdom or in eternity. Instead this is speaking of the believers' current *potential* conditions: either they can be pressing on to maturity, or they can be fallen alongside. This context (and that of 5:12-14) is a parallel to Paul's expression of the four types of people in 1 Corinthians – the natural man (2:14), the infant (3:1), the fleshly man (3:1), and the spiritual man (2:15). The natural man is not in view in Hebrews 6:1-8. The fleshly man is, practically speaking, in the same place as the infant, and should be pressing on to maturity as the spiritual man is. Incidentally, these terms are all used in the context of how one responds to truth. The

---

[149] Grant Osborne, "A Classical Arminian View" in *Four Views on the Warning Passages in Hebrews*, Herbert Bateman, Gen Ed. (Grand Rapids, MI: Kregel, 2007), 128.

natural man *can't* receive truth, the infant *hasn't* yet moved beyond elementary aspects of truth, the fleshly man *won't* move beyond elementary aspects of truth, and the spiritual man *is* moving beyond elementary aspects of truth, pressing toward maturity.

10:19-31

The calls to action are that we should draw towards (v.22, *proserchomai*), hold fast the confession (v.23, *katechomen ten homologian*), and consider (v. 24, *katanoomen*) how to stimulate one another to love and good deeds. These things are contrasted to a continual purposeful sinning after receiving the full knowledge (*epignosin*) of the truth (10:26), for which the negative consequence are (1) there no longer for sin remains a sacrifice, but (2) some have a fearful awaiting of judgment. If considered on its own, this context could be understood to imply that only those who continue in sin expect judgment, however, the writer is building on a previous context in which judgment comes to *all* after death (9:27). The issue is what that judgment will bring. In the case of the one continuing purposefully in sin, there is no other sacrifice besides that of Christ, so if one continues in sin (or having fallen alongside, as was described in 6:1-8), there is no alternative path whereby one can pursue their walk with God. Instead, the behavior deserves a severe punishment (10:29). Severity in judgment is deserved because of God's character, as illustrated in 10:26-31, but also because the person in sinfulness tramples the blood of Christ, and insults the Spirit of grace (10:29). The continually and purposefully sinning believer offends all three persons of the triune God. Note the parallel between this passage and Ephesians 1.

In Ephesians 1:4-6, the Father has predestined and chosen believers to be in Christ, yet in Hebrews 10:26-31 He is a terrifying judge. In Ephesians 1:7-12 the Son redeems through His blood, and in Hebrews 10:29 He and His blood are being trampled. In Ephesians 1:13-14 the Spirit seals and guarantees the believer's position, and in Hebrews 10:29 that same Spirit is insulted. In Ephesians 1, all three Persons are acting to secure the position of the believer, in Hebrews 10, the continually and purposefully sinning believer is fighting God on all three fronts. While the writer reminds that it is a terrifying thing to fall into the hands of the living God (10:31), he also concludes this broad context by adding that we are not of a withdrawal unto destruction, but of a faith unto the possession of soul (10:39). No matter how we fight against God, because of His work, and because of the faith which He used to accomplish our position (Eph 2:8-9, 1 Pet 1:3-5), we will not become those of a withdrawal unto destruction, because we are of a faith unto life.

Nonetheless, the exhortation is clear: draw towards, hold fast, consider. These are all ongoing practical aspects of life in Christ, and the writer of Hebrews is careful to tell readers that while failure might result in deserving a different destiny, believers simply don't have one. What is affected is the process of growth. This warning passage is not addressing unbelievers, nor is it warning believers of loss of salvation. There is no statement of loss at all, only a reminder to act in a way that does not throw away our confidence, which has in itself great reward (10:35).

12:14-17

In this context, the call to action is to pursue peace (with all) and holiness (12:14), and the first negative consequence is that without (at least) that particular holiness no one would see the Lord. That the definite article precedes the term *holiness* helps readers understand that this isn't holiness in general, but a specific component or kind of holiness that is necessary in order to see the Lord. What would that be? In 10:10 the *we* were made holy (perfect tense, *hegiasmenoi*), and in 12:10 He disciplines the *we* so that we would share or take with us His holiness (*hagiotetes*). It is important to recognize that the holiness required in 12:14 (*hagiasmon*) is already possessed by the *we*. Thus the pursuit of that holiness is either the same kind of pursuit as is evident in holding more emphatically to what is already held (as in 2:1-3), or the *we* who have that holiness are to pursue that holiness for those who *don't* have it as part of strengthening hands that are weak and knees that are feeble (12:12). In either of these understandings, the practical progress or lack thereof has no implications effecting the position or destiny of the believer.

On the other side of the argument, if a person has that particular kind of holiness, the implication is that they will indeed see the Lord. There are no degrees of quality or location in seeing the Lord. One either sees the Lord, or doesn't, and the determining factor is the holiness – which the *we* already have. It is because of that possession of holiness that 12:12 assumes the audience had the ability to strengthen others.

Now, if the pursuit of holiness is in the same sense of holding to it more emphatically, then the issue might be a personal practice that *reflects* the believer's position. But if the pursuit of holiness is to pursue positional holiness in those who don't have it, then part of that pursuit may include overseeing (or seeing to it) that some are not lacking in the grace of God (12:15).

The illustration in 12:16-17 portrays a person (Esau) who traded something cheaply and couldn't get it back, regardless of how much it was desired. That negative consequence is analogous to the negative consequences mentioned in 12:15 – lacking or coming short in God's grace in the present tense (*husteron*), and root of bitterness sprouting in the present tense (*phuousa*). This analogy does not extend far enough for the reader to *textually* conclude that the negative consequence is an eschatological one.

The evangelistic view would not work with this passage in light of the *we* having holiness. The loss of salvation view could be supported *if* the holiness needed to be pursued because it could be lost. Neither this context nor the broader cumulative case being made by the writer provides any exegetical evidence that holiness can be lost. Likewise, the loss of status understanding seems untenable in any case here. Either one does or does not see the Lord. If there is any loss of status here, it would seem to be necessarily a loss of salvation, and that seems incompatible with the broader case the writer of Hebrews is making.

13:4-6

This passage is not typically counted as one of the warning passages, but because it contains the three warning passage ingredients (exhortation, connective, negative consequence), it is included here. The call to action is that marriage is to be considered as honorable, and the sexual relationship undefiled. Those who do not fulfill this (immoral ones and adulterers) God will judge (*krinei*). Because this passage doesn't specify what the judgment entails, this passage doesn't support or eliminate any of the four views, though 13:1-

2 make it fairly clear that the antecedent of the second person plural in 13:4-6 is believers, and ultimately includes the *we* of previous contexts.

Conclusion

It seems evident that in each case, these warning passages are addressed to believers. If this observation is accurate, then the evangelistic interpretation of these passages is not viable. It also seems evident that in none of these passages is positional or eschatological salvation in danger. If that is accurate, then the loss of salvation and loss of status views are not viable. Further, it seems evident that cumulatively these warning passages focus on believers who may at times be deserving of judgment, but are instead met with God's discipline (12:7-11), which results in the peaceful fruit of righteousness.

While 1 Corinthians 3:12-15 speaks unmistakably about believers' loss of rewards in a future judgment, that theological truth does not seem to be the focus of the writer of Hebrews. Believers' loss of rewards is a real possibility, but it seems to not be advocated (or addressed at all) in the warning passages of Hebrews.

Instead of motivating believers to progress by loss of position, or by loss of future status, the writer of Hebrews seems to motivate believers to progress by describing what the loss of progress looks like. The device is similar to that invoked by Paul when he challenges believers to "not be conformed to the image of this world, but be transformed by the renewing of your mind, so that you may prove what the will of God is, that which is good, acceptable, and perfect" (Rom 12:2). Such progress is only reasonable (Rom 12:1), and it is the expectation for every believer. Without that progress, we will find ourselves walking as fleshly believers (1 Cor 3:3).

The exhortation of Hebrews is to believers who "should be teachers by now" (5:12), but who have need again of the basics and of milk. The Hebrew believers need, once again, the food of infants (5:13), as they have not advanced to the point of being able to stomach food for the mature (5:14). Their need is not to fix their position or to protect some aspect of their future standing with God, but rather it is to grow up – to mature in Christ. Likewise, as we seek to grow to maturity ourselves, let us not motivate ourselves or others by placing upon anyone a yoke of fearing the loss of what God has already guaranteed. Instead, perhaps we can challenge ourselves and others to simply grow up – for that is ultimately what children are designed to do.

10
PRIORITY OF HERMENEUTICS IN GENRE DETERMINATIONS:
THE GENRE OF GENESIS 1

The Bible contains four basic genres of literature: historical narrative, poetry, prophetic, and epistolary. The genre classification of Genesis 1 is very important for our understanding of the overall message of Scripture, because the chapter deals with so many foundational details, including the character of God, the nature of creation, and the backdrop for how we understand sin and redemption.

For example, in Genesis 1:26-28 God is recorded as having a very important conversation with Himself. If this conversation literally happened, then the passage is an early and potent evidence for the concept of the triunity of the Godhead. On the other hand, if the conversation can be dismissed as figurative language – as anthropomorphism, for example – then perhaps we would not conclude that the conversation actually happened, but that it was instead simply a poetic expression.

Clearly Genesis 1 is neither prophetic nor epistolary, as it makes no statements regarding the future beyond its immediate context, nor is it addressed to any particular recipients. So the genre question regarding Genesis 1 is between historical narrative and Hebrew poetry. That Genesis 1 is

Hebrew poetry is a fairly common view, but not necessarily because of the literary characteristics of the chapter, but rather because of the quality of the propositions made – huge statements, for sure. But does this chapter contain enough actual poetic characteristics to be considered poetry, or is it more obviously historical narrative?

Hebrew poetry is discernible by a number of literary devices – especially parallelism (the repetition of one thing in two or more different ways). Parallelism is evident in passages like Psalm 119:105: "Your word is a lamp to my feet and a light to my path" (NASB). What is particularly striking about Hebrew poetic parallelism is that it usually occurs within close proximities – in other words, within narrow, rather than broad contexts.

Genesis 1 lacks these parallelisms. There are certainly propositions connected by the Hebrew *vav*, which often functions as the English conjunction *and*. But in each of these cases in Genesis 1, the propositions following the conjunctions are not poetic restatements of the earlier propositions, but rather communicate resulting conditions of the earlier propositions. To illustrate, let's examine each *vav* conjunction in the first 5 verses, represented by the English and in the list below.

1:1 heavens *and* the earth – two different entities, no restatement.

1:2 and the earth was – prefixes the noun, followed by a verb, no restatement.

1:2 formless *and* void – without form and empty, two distinct characteristics, no restatement.

1:2 and darkness was over the surface of the waters – not a restatement, having nothing to do with the previous descriptions, but adding detail.

1:2 and the Spirit of God was moving over the surface of the waters. – unless we are to understand that the darkness and the Spirit of God are synonymous, then there is no parallelism here either.

1:3 and God said – again, followed by a new verb, no restatement.

1:3 and there was light – followed by distinct verb, a result of the former statement, not a restatement of it.

1:4 and God saw – new verb describing God's action.

1:4 and God separated – verb distinct from that of the previous proposition (separating is not a restatement of seeing).

1:5 and God called the light day

1:5 and the darkness He called night

1:5 and there was evening

1:5 and there was morning – in none of the four instances of the *vav* in verse 5 is there restatement of a previous proposition.

These samples reveal no correspondence to Hebrew poetry at all, and provide no data that should cause an interpreter to conclude against a face-value classification of Genesis 1 as historical narrative.

It is also helpful to note an important grammatical principle of Biblical Hebrew: a literary device called the *vav* consecutive. When the first verb is in the perfect tense and subsequent verbs are imperfect, the *vavs* are consecutive, and denote a continuous narrative in the past. (Incidentally, in prophetic literature, there is continuous narrative referring to the future, which is indicated by the first verb in the imperfect, and subsequent verbs in the narrative in the perfect.) Let's take a quick look at the verbs in these same five verses.

1:1 (*bara*, created) – perfect

1:2 (*hayetah*, it was) – perfect
1:2 (*merakepet*, was hovering) – piel intensive

1:3 (*wayyomer*, and He said) – imperfect
1:3 (*yehiy*, let there be) – imperfect
1:3 (*yehiy*, and there was) – imperfect

1:4 (*yereh*, and saw) – imperfect
1:4 (*wayabedel*, and caused to be divided) – hiphil imperfect

1:5 (*wayiqerah*, and called) –imperfect
1:5 (*qarah*, called) – perfect
1:5 (*wayehiy*, and it was) – imperfect
1:5 (*wayehiy*, and it was) – imperfect

Verse 1 makes a statement, that God created the heavens and the earth. Verse 2 introduces an explicative narrative, with *vav* consecutives up to the middle of verse 5. The perfect verb in verse 5 is followed by *vav* consecutives with the time stamp (it was evening and it was morning one day). Simply put, the series and placement of *vav* consecutives and time stamps makes this a series of historical narratives.

In short there are several overwhelming evidences that Genesis 1 is historical narrative and not poetic:

- Genesis 1 does not contain the parallelism that is characteristic of Hebrew poetry.
- Genesis 1 does contain repeated instances of the *vav* consecutive, indicating continuous narrative of the past.
- Further, Genesis 1 does also contain sequential time stamps (evening and morning, one day, second day, etc.)

The text of Genesis 1, taken at face value, should be recognized as historical narrative and not poetic. This is very significant for our understanding of the things discussed in Genesis 1. The question then is whether or not the Genesis account is historically true, not whether or not the author was trying to communicate something other than historical material. If true, then the heavens and earth were created as described, and what follows in Genesis is grounded on the platform of historicity. What we understand from the Biblical record about God's character, humanity, sin, and salvation is reliable and based on an assertion of historical truth.

11
PRIORITY OF HERMENEUTICS IN GENRE DETERMINATIONS:
THE RESURRECTION AND GRECO-ROMAN BIOS

The resurrection of Jesus Christ is one of three major components of the Gospel, described by Paul in 1 Corinthians 15:3-4: "...that Christ died for our sins according to the Scriptures, and that He was buried, and that He was raised on the third day according to the Scriptures..."

While the death may be the central component, since it was by His death as our substitute that He paid the price to the Father for our sin (both inherited and committed), His burial evidenced the legitimacy of His death, and His resurrection evidenced the legitimacy of His substitutionary work on the cross. The resurrection declared with power that He was indeed the Son of God (Rom 1:4), and the Jews of Jesus' day understand that His claim to be *the* Son of God was a messianic claim to be God Himself (see Jn 8:24-25, 28-30, 56-59 [Is 48:12,16; Rev 22:13-14, 16]). The resurrection, then was an important evidence of who Jesus was and therefore that His death was efficacious and not empty.

Paul describes the resurrection as the key component of the Gospel, since that event confirms the other components. He further explains that if Christ has not been raised from the dead, we are fools to be pitied, we are hopeless, and we are even blasphemers (1 Cor 15:12-19). Consequently, the resurrection of Jesus is the pivot point for all of Christianity. If Christ was raised, His message and work is confirmed, if not, then all who believe in Him as the Bible prescribes (e.g., Jn 3:16) are simply misguided idiots at best.

In arguing for the historicity of the resurrection, Michael Licona attempts to compare five naturalistic theories of the resurrection (offering non-supernatural explanations for what happened to Jesus) with the theory that the resurrection was in fact historic.[150] In this specific enterprise, Licona does a commendable job, concluding that the historical resurrection theory is more historically sound than the other five naturalistic theories. The detail and painstaking scholarship evident in the development of his arguments is exemplary in many aspects.

However, I would argue that in his work there is a significant methodological flaw that undermines his case. I cite this defect as a cautionary tale, but before I examine this problem in some detail, I must first warn the reader not to throw out the proverbial baby with the bathwater. Licona does some excellent work here, and I hope his efforts serve as a springboard for other Biblical scholars to fill in the gaps left by his work. As an overall project – as a scholarly and objective presentation of the arguments for and against the historicity of Jesus' resurrection, this work is worthy. Nonetheless, the methodological flaw is perhaps fatal to his case, and at least undermines the authority of his primary sources (the canonical Gospels). Further, it is worth noting that this methodological device assumed and employed by Licona is gaining in popularity and influence. Consequently, I believe it worthwhile to discuss

---

[150] Michael Licona, *The Resurrection of Jesus: A New Historiographical Approach* (Downers Grove, IL: IVP, 2010), 465-610.

in this forum the device, and encourage the reader to investigate and conclude on the matter.

First, Licona commendably builds a case for his methodology, asking, ""What does it mean when historians say that a particular event occurred?"[151] He argues for the importance of objectivity in the historiographical process, citing "horizons" as preunderstanding that can often impede the objective pursuit of truth in historical matters.[152] He describes that historians have a responsibility to manage their horizons by being transparent about them, and by attention to method, but even then complete objectivity is elusive.[153] With that caveat, he agrees with Richard Evans definition of a historical fact as "something that happened and that historians attempt to 'discover' through verification procedures,"[154] and he is transparent in his employment of that definition. He further describes the method employed as methodical neutrality, "where the one making the claim bears the burden of proof,"[155] and further suggests that "historians....speak of the probable truth of a theory rather than absolute certainty. Historical conclusions are provisional."[156]

It is evident at this point that there will be some friction between Licona's historiography and the idea of inerrancy. Whereas Licona's historical method demands only a provisional understanding of truth, it would seem his Biblical theology would demand a very different approach. Where these two concepts collide, there is a decision to be made as to what

---

[151] Ibid., 30.
[152] Ibid., 39.
[153] Ibid., 50-62.
[154] Ibid., 93.
[155] Ibid., 96 and 99.
[156] Ibid., 103.

interpretation of the data is to be preferred. This subtle tension has not –so- subtle results as Licona explains his interpretation of the Gospel data, and as he underscores his rationalistic preference for historiography over theology. He admits candidly, "While I believe that the occasional feelings I have experienced of closeness with God may be authentic, I am aware that they may also be the result of long-term conditioning and expectations...For me, if the resurrection of Jesus were ever disproved, I would feel compelled to abandon my Christian faith and remain a theist with no commitments to a particular view."[157]

Now, I must be careful here not to misrepresent Licona, as he makes it clear in the following pages that he does not believe the resurrection *can* be disproven (though he does admit that he is open to the possibility that the historical evidence might not be strong enough to conclude the resurrection is *historical*[158]), and on the contrary he concludes with great confidence that the resurrection is historical, rather than a fiction. I don't mention these passages to suggest doubt on his part; rather I think they are important as they betray a preference for historiography over and against the Biblical data as inspired. In other words, if I understand Licona's case correctly, it seems he values first determining historicity, and then appreciating its doctrinal value. This order of priority has significant hermeneutic consequences, as we will see. The question arises: What if historicity cannot be determined beyond the immediate claims of a particular text? How this question is answered in Licona's work underscores what I believe is the fundamental flaw in the method employed.

---

[157] Ibid., 130-131.
[158] Ibid., 131.

PRIORITY OF HERMENEUTICS IN GENRE: THE RESURRECTION 139

One such passage, described as "a strange little text,"[159] for which there is no external historical verification is Matthew 27:52-53. This passage describes the bodily resurrection and post-resurrection ministries of saints in Jerusalem at the time of Christ's death. Licona explains (away) this passage as follows:

> Given the presence of phenomenological language used in a symbolic manner in both Jewish and Roman literature related to a major event such as the death of an emperor or the end of a reigning king or even a kingdom, the presence of ambiguity in the relevant text of Ignatius, and that so very little can be known about Thallus's comment on the darkness…it seems to me that an understanding of the language of Matthew 27:52-53 as "special effects" with eschatological Jewish texts and thought in mind is most plausible.[160]

Special effects. Since the events in these verses are historically unverifiable, their literal interpretation (as historical fact) is implausible, and consequently redefined as special effects. How does Licona arrive at this conclusion?

Licona spent nearly five-hundred pages describing with transparency the method he would employ in weighing the hypotheses. But very early on, he inserts a very pivotal statement: "There is somewhat of a consensus among contemporary scholars that the Gospels belong to the genre of Greco-Roman biography (*bios*). *Bioi* offered the ancient biographer great flexibility for rearranging material and inventing speeches in order to communicate the teachings,

---
[159] Ibid., 548.
[160] Ibid., 552.

philosophy, and political beliefs of the subject, and they often included legend. Because *bios* was a flexible genre, it is often difficult to determining where history ends and legend begins."[161]

And there it is. *Bios* is flexible. Some of it can be historical, other aspects can be mere special effects. On this point, Licona offers a lengthy footnote and further refers to pp. 201-208,[162] in which he defers in particular to Richard Burridge, who writes,

> The genre of Bios is flexible and diverse, with variation in the pattern of features from one Bios to another. The gospels also diverge from the pattern in some aspects, but no to any greater degree than other *Bioi*; in other words, they have at least as much in common with Graeco0Roman *Bioi*, as the *Biois* have with each other. Therefore the Gospels must belong to the genre of *Bios*.[163]

Burridge is also transparent about the hermeneutic implications of this genre assumption:

> Finally, we have outlined some generic and hermeneutical implications of this result. The four canonical gospels belong together as *Bioi Iesou*, unlike the non-canonical gospels, many of which have lost the

---

[161] Ibid., 34.
[162] In these pages it is seems especially evident as well that Licona is comfortable with the Q theory, a position that is symptomatic of the methodological flaw I am describing.
[163] Richard Burridge, *What Are the Gospels? A Comparison With Graeco-Roman Biography*, 2nd. Ed. (Grand Rapids, MI: Eerdmans, 2004), 250.

generic features of *Bios*. Furthermore, nothing in the social setting of the gospel texts, writers and audiences prevents them being interpreted as *Bioi*. Finally, this genre of Bios has distinct hermeneutical implications for the gospel studies, reaffirming the centrality of the person of Jesus of Nazareth."[164]

Burridge admits that the genre classification is difficult to prove, but is very useful. He observes, "It has become clear in this study that the narrower the genre proposed for the gospels, the harder it is to prove the case, but the more useful the hermeneutic implications."[165]

In these passages, Burridge admits several important points: (1) the canonical Gospels share some similarities, but also have key differences, (2) while there is nothing that prevents their genre classification, there is also nothing that requires it, (3) there are significant hermeneutic implications, and (4) those hermeneutic implications are pragmatic ones. Specifically, it seems the *Bios* genre classification allows the interpreter to arbitrarily cast aside certain aspects of the text as long as we don't cast aside the centrality of Jesus.

To his credit Licona anticipates the question this begs. He notes, "If some or all of the phenomena reported at Jesus' death are poetic devices, we may rightly ask whether Jesus' resurrection is not more of the same."[166] He offers two brief arguments against that conclusion (no indication of early poetic interpretations, and no known early opponents of Christianity

---

[164] Ibid., 250-251.
[165] Ibid., 247.
[166] Licona, 553.

critiqued on the basis of misunderstanding poetry as history)[167] Despite these two points, I believe the damage has been done. Burridge uses the *Bios* classification in the same way Philo utilized allegorical interpretation – to redeem the Scriptures from rationalistic critiques. By adopting the *Bios* theory, Licona is participating in genre override, which allows for explaining away difficult passages, via a menu approach to historicity in the Gospel events.

Admittedly, for a historian who adopts Licona's historiographical presuppositions, Matthew 27:52-5 is problematic because (1) it sounds implausible, and (2) there is no external historical verification. To resolve the difficulty by changing a genre classification creates a far greater problem, precisely due to the hermeneutic implications Burridge identified. Such a hermeneutic move is useful for resolving isolated difficulties, but *it is also useful for undermining the authority of the entire text.* If it is implausible that people could be resurrected at the death of Christ, then it would seem equally implausible that Jesus should be the Son of God – even God Himself – and should be raised from the dead. As Licona admits, if any of the text is legend, it becomes difficult to know where the legend ends and the history begins. What he may view as history, I may view as legend, and he has made the case for my understanding-as-legend to be legitimate. And if the Gospel writers had the flexibility of inventing speeches, how can I have any certainty about what Jesus said? Sometimes "useful" can be the enemy of truth (e.g., Gen 3:6).

Why not view the Gospels not as *Bios*, which is so nebulous as to defy definition and certainty, and instead view

---

[167] Ibid.

them simply as historical narrative – which even Burridge admits is possible (at least if only by implication)? After all, should Matthew be viewed as a totally different genre than Luke, who described his work as "the exact truth?" (*asphaleia* – certainty, Lk 1:4)? Why not take the writers at face value? Granted if we do so, we are stuck with these pesky resurrection narratives that we can't *historically* verify – and which still look foolish to skeptics no matter our historiographical method.

12
PRIORITY OF HERMENEUTICS IN GENRE DETERMINATIONS:
REVELATION AND APOCALYPTIC LITERATURE

It may seem odd to suggest that the book entitled *Apocalupsis* does not belong to the genre of literature commonly referred to as apocalyptic, nonetheless that is my suggestion here. The term employed in the title of the book denotes a revelation or disclosure.[168] While this particular *revealing* or *disclosing* describes a broad swathe of eschatological events, it is not its own literary genre.

Apocalyptic as a genre is described as "characteristically pseudonymous; it takes narrative form, employs esoteric language, expresses a pessimistic view of the present, and treats the final events as imminent."[169] Henry Barclay Swete (Cambridge), even while arguing that Revelation is apocalyptic literature, admits that the book differs from that genre, in that the book of Revelation (1) is not pseudepigraphic, (2) it engages a specific audience [i.e., seven churches], (3) has a significant church focus, rather than a purely Israel nation-centered focus, and (4) includes notes of insight and foresight that are more

---

[168] BDAG, 2nd Edition, 114.
[169] Robert Lerner, "apocalyptic language" at Brittanica.com, viewed 5/21/2014.

indicative of inspiration than is found in earlier extra-Biblical apocalyptic literature.[170]

Despite these differences between Revelation and extra-Biblical apocalyptic literature, Swete considered the gift of revelation to be not entirely the same as the gift of prophecy, and thus revelation stood distinct as a particular manifestation of the spirit,[171] "in which the spirit of the prophet seemed to be carried up into a higher sphere, endowed for the time with new powers of vision, and enabled to hear words which could not be reproduced in the terms of human thought, or could be reproduced only through the medium of symbolic imagery."[172]

The irony of Swete's commentary here is that in footnote he appeals to 1 Corinthians 12:4, a passage in which Paul describes words heard in the third heaven which man is not permitted to speak. However, in Revelation, John is given a direct commission to record all of what he sees. Further, in 1:3 and 22:18 there are blessings and warnings for those who hear the words written in the prophecy, and we read seven times in chapters 2-3 and once again in 13:7 the repeated refrain, "he who has an ear, let him hear..." In the first seven instances, the content is expressly, "what the Spirit says to the churches."

As for the gift of revelation as a unique manifestation of the Spirit, no such gift is evident in Revelation (or anywhere else in the NT, for that matter). Swete appeals to Ephesians 1:17 as in instance of the "gift of spiritual vision,"[173] and while the passage indeed uses the noun (ἀποκαλύψεως), it is in the context

---

[170] Henry Barclay Swete, *The Apocalypse of John, Third Edition* (London: MacMillan and Co., 1911), xxviii-xxx.
[171] Ibid., xxiii.
[172] Ibid.
[173] Ibid., xxii.

of a request made on behalf of all believers (or at least all believers in Ephesus at the time). In short, Paul is not requesting that believers be granted a mystical gift (in the sense Swete employs the term – as an ability), but that believers be granted a spirit of wisdom and revelation in the knowledge of Christ. This deeper, more mature understanding of Christ seems Paul's common expectation for all believers, not some mystical enlightenment for only an elite few.

While the unsurprising dissimilarities between Revelation and extra-Biblical apocalyptic literature are convincing enough to this writer that Revelation should not be considered a part of the apocalyptic genre, the internal genre-identification is dispositive. Revelation 1:3 and 22:7, 10, 18, and 19 all refer to the writing as prophecy. The final reference in 22:19 is to the book of this the prophecy (τοῦ βιβλίου τῆς προφητείας ταύτης). It is evident that the use of the term revelation or unveiling (Ἀποκάλυψις) in 1:1 is not a genre-technical term, but is rather an explanation of the content of the prophecy: the revealing of Jesus Christ.

The genre placement of the book has significant hermeneutic implications – in fact, the interpretation of the book is pre-determined by the genre classification. If the book fits in the apocalyptic genre, then we shouldn't expect it to be understood literally at all. An apocalyptic genre placement would support the preterist interpretation (a non-literal view that the events were fulfilled during the first century), the historicist or continuist interpretation (a non-literal approach that views the book as describing events in the church between the apostolic age and the second coming of Christ), the idealist interpretation (a non-literal view that the book doesn't predict actual events at all, but rather symbolizes the epic struggle between good and evil), and the eclectic interpretation (a hybrid approach, popularized by George Ladd, this view combines the preterist and futurist interpretation).

On the other hand, only the futurist model (a literal interpretation in which the events described in the book, beyond chapters 2-3, are still yet in the future) is supported by the simple genre classification of the book as prophecy. The futuristic interpretive model is the only one of the five models that stems from the literal grammatical historical hermeneutic, and is initially derived from the simple past-present-future commission of John in Revelation 1:19: "Therefore, write the things which you have seen, and the things which are, and the things which will take place after these things."

It should come as no surprise that those who prefer a non-literal interpretation of the book would also gravitate toward the apocalyptic classification, but it is surprising how many futurist interpreters likewise follow their non-literal colleagues in the apocalyptic classification. Instead of blindly accepting terminology that undermines the literal grammatical historical hermeneutic, perhaps we should take our cue from the pages of Scripture and call the book what it is: *prophecy* – a prophecy regarding the unveiling of Christ, and which is largely about "the things which will take place after these things."

13
PRIORITY OF HERMENEUTICS IN METAPHYSICS:
THE HERMENEUTIC ROOTS OF OUR SOTERIOLOGICAL CRISIS

Failing to recognize that the Reformation's hermeneutic inconsistency obscured more than just eschatology and ecclesiology, dispensationalists happily built upon the platform of Reformed soteriology. In failing to ascertain a purely Biblical soteriology, we (dispensationalists) became *systems* theologians, rather than *Biblical* ones. We perceived it was permissible and even profitable to construct a (dispensational) system that incorporated seemingly positive aspects of Reformed theology, as long as we rejected those conclusions that were incompatible with our new system. We defended the system with inconsistencies borrowed from the Reformers and from their spiritual fathers. Unwittingly we have built upon a framework so shifty that further construction yields fatal cracks if not addressed with a total reconstruction.

The soteriological controversies of the past thirty years represent attempts to resolve the methodological discord. And while it seems we are oft focused on critiquing the resulting *conclusions* — especially Lordship salvation on the one hand, and hyper-grace on the other, we give little attention to *the methods that give rise to these doctrines*, and perhaps even less attention to the *other doctrines* the methods derive. We have long understood that there is a distinctly dispensational eschatology, but we must also realize that there is a distinctly dispensational soteriology. In fact, dispensationalism is not a system focused on only a few representative topics, but it should be a vibrant and comprehensive result of understanding the whole Bible through the literal grammatical historical lens. If dispensationalism is not a Biblically accurate explanatory device, then its worth is lost and it becomes merely another system to which we pledge our loyalties, with no good reason for preferring it over competing systems.

Historically, soteriology has been heavily guided by *systems*, and provides fertile ground for case studies in methodology. The discussion that follows considers the role that hermeneutics plays in soteriology, considering 1 Corinthians 6:9 as a case study, in order to help us engage contemporary challenges in soteriology, and especially Lordship salvation. The outcomes in handling this passage remind us that our conclusions should be exegetically rather than theologically derived.

Considering 1 Corinthians 6:9-11

> **9** Or do you not know that the unrighteous will not inherit the kingdom of God? Do not be deceived; neither fornicators, nor idolaters, nor adulterers, nor effeminate, nor homosexuals, **10** nor thieves, nor *the* covetous, nor drunkards, nor revilers, nor swindlers, will inherit the kingdom of God. **11** Such were some of you; but you were washed, but you were sanctified, but you were justified in the name of the Lord Jesus Christ and in the Spirit of our

God.

9 Ἢ οὐκ οἴδατε ὅτι ἄδικοι θεοῦ βασιλείαν οὐ κληρονομήσουσιν; μὴ πλανᾶσθε· οὔτε πόρνοι οὔτε εἰδωλολάτραι οὔτε μοιχοὶ οὔτε μαλακοὶ οὔτε ἀρσενοκοῖται **10** οὔτε κλέπται οὔτε πλεονέκται, οὐ μέθυσοι, οὐ λοίδοροι, οὐχ ἅρπαγες βασιλείαν θεοῦ κληρονομήσουσιν. **11** καὶ ταῦτά τινες ἦτε· ἀλλὰ ἀπελούσασθε, ἀλλὰ ἡγιάσθητε, ἀλλὰ ἐδικαιώθητε ἐν τῷ ὀνόματι τοῦ κυρίου Ἰησοῦ Χριστοῦ καὶ ἐν τῷ πνεύματι τοῦ θεοῦ ἡμῶν.[174]

In this passage Paul challenges the Corinthian believers to a walk that is more becoming of a believer than the Corinthian behavior of brother going to law against brother. The exegetical pivot point here is whether *the unrighteous* (ἄδικοι) refers to those of unrighteous *position* or *practice (or both)*. If it refers to individuals of a particular position, then the *unrighteous* are unbelievers, and there is little complexity in the idea that unbelievers will not inherit the kingdom of God. However, if the term is unrelated to position and instead refers to practice, then there are significant questions to address.

If Paul is using the term *homosexuals* as a sample of the actions engaged by the unrighteous, then he is not making any soteriological statement at all, until verse 11, in which he describes the Corinthians as being characterized by these behaviors prior to their salvation. On the other hand, if Paul is describing those who are homosexuals as *the unrighteous* – and thus *unbelievers by definition*, then there is a soteriological

---

[174] Barbara Aland, Kurt Aland, Matthew Black et al., *The Greek New Testament*, 4th ed., 449 (Federal Republic of Germany: United Bible Societies, 1993).

implication in 6:9-10: that one must cease these actions in order to be washed, sanctified, and justified. Simply put, the question is this: does a person first receive washing, sanctification, and justification and then have the ability to demonstrate changed behavior, or are they first expected to change their behavior in order to qualify for the washing, sanctification, and justification.

Notice the *practical* emphasis by some notable interpreters. John Calvin observes that,

> [T]he unrighteous, then, that is, those who inflict injury on their brethren, who defraud or circumvent others, who, in short, are intent upon their own advantage at the expense of injuring others, will not inherit the kingdom of God...The wicked, then, do inherit the kingdom of God, but it is only in the event of their having been first converted to the Lord in true repentance, and having in this way ceased to be wicked...The simple meaning, therefore, is this, that prior to their being regenerated by grace, some of the Corinthians were covetous, others adulterers, others extortioners, others effeminate, others revilers, but now, being made free by Christ, they were such no longer.[175]

To Charles Hodge, *the unrighteous* are basically those who break God's laws:

> The *unrighteous* in this immediate connection, means the unjust; those who violate the principles of justice in their dealings with their fellow-men. It is not the unjust alone,

---

[175] John Calvin, *Commentary on Corinthians, Vol I* (Grand Rapids, MI: CCEL, 1999), 126-129.

however, who are to be thus debarred from the Redeemer's kingdom — but also those who break any of the commandments of God, as this and other passages of Scripture distinctly teach.[176]

To Adam Clarke,

> [T]he unrighteous, αδικοι, those who act contrary to right, cannot inherit, for the inheritance is by right. He who is not a child of God has no right to the family inheritance, for that inheritance is for the children. If children, then heirs; heirs of God, and joint heirs with Christ, Romans 8:17. There are here ten classes of transgressors which the apostle excludes from the kingdom of God; and any man who is guilty of any one of the evils mentioned above is thereby excluded from this kingdom, whether it imply the Church of Christ here below, or the state of glory hereafter.[177]

In John Piper's estimation, "the unrepentant practice of homosexual behavior (like other sins) will exclude a person from the kingdom of God... (1 Corinthians 6:9-10)."[178]

In each of these comments, the interpreters conclude in favor of the practical view of *the unrighteous*. The unrighteous

---

[176] Charles Hodge, *An Exposition of 1 Corinthians*, (Albany, OR: AGES Software, 1997), 121.
[177] Adam Clarke, Commentary on 1 Corinthians, viewed at http://www.studylight.org/com/acc/view.cgi?book=1co&chapter=006 on 10/13/2013.
[178] John Piper, "The Tornado, the Lutherans, and Homosexuality" at http://www.desiringgod.org/blog/posts/the-tornado-the-lutherans-and-homosexuality, 8/19/2009.

are *those who do unrighteous things*, In order to be washed, sanctified, and justified, there must be some resolution with regard to the actions that exclude the actor from the kingdom of God. John MacArthur's Lordship salvation view accounts for that resolution by asserting that a person must repent from (by which he means *to turn away from*) his or her sin,[179] and that person must be submitted to the Lordship of Christ in order to receive washing, sanctification, and justification.[180] But in examining MacArthur's understanding of 1 Corinthians 6:9, an interesting progression over time is evident. In a 1975 message on 1 Corinthians 6:9-11, MacArthur handles the passage exegetically, and concludes in favor of the positional approach to *the unrighteous*:

> The unregenerate, it says very clearly people that in verse 9, these are unrighteous people. And in verse 11 it says "Such were some of you before you were saved." So we know it's talking about unsaved people. People who were unregenerate and didn't know God…This passage is not teaching that if a Christian every does any of these things he'll lose his salvation, it's simply categorizing the world and saying you used to be one of those kind…And a new life demands a new lifestyle.[181]

---

[179] John MacArthur, *The Gospel According to Jesus, Revised and Expanded* (Grand Rapids, MI: Zondervan, 1994), 178.
[180] John MacArthur, *The Gospel According to Jesus, Revised and Expanded* (Grand Rapids, MI: Zondervan, 1994), 34-36, 192, 221.
[181] John MacArthur "Forgive Because You're Forgiven: 1 Corinthians 6:9-11, at http://www.gty.org/resources/sermons/1826/forgive-because-youre-forgiven, 11/02/1975.

But notice that in later handlings of the same passage, MacArthur abandons that textual argument in favor of a theological argument. This is evidence of a substantial drift in MacArthur's hermeneutic method.

In a 2012 message on 1 Corinthians 6:9-11, MacArthur says of homosexuals, "these people practice a sin which excludes them from the kingdom of God."[182] "They will never belong to God's kingdom as long as they continue to live in that lifestyle."[183] In that same message, after quoting extensively from Deuteronomy and Leviticus in order to cite homosexuality as an abomination, MacArthur observes that Christ did not end the Law, He fulfilled it. MacArthur adds that "God's moral law is unchanging and absolutely unchangeable."[184] Notice one significant result of MacArthur's hermeneutic shift is an inconsistency in applying the Law. He suggests that those laws are still binding today, but he disregards the legislated penalties (which are part of that law) for sexual crimes committed under the Mosaic Law. In doing so, MacArthur is exegetically inconsistent and ignores the progress or revelation, the distinction between Israel and the church, and the distinctions in the administrations of God. Rather than justify the sinfulness of homosexuality from passages outside the context of Mosaic Law, he is placing under the Law the church and even all unbelievers – two groups that were never under the Mosaic Law.

MacArthur's employment of the theological hermeneutic (or, reading a theological position into the Biblical text) is

---

[182] John MacArthur, "Thinking Biblically About Homosexuality (1 Cor 6:9-10)" at http://www.youtube.com/watch?v=udT-Ejqwi84, 21:23.)
[183] Ibid., 21:41.
[184] Ibid., 40:55.

evidenced also in his direct affirmations of Lordship salvation. In 1994 he lamented that,

> The church's witness to the world has been sacrificed on the altar of cheap grace....The promise of eternal life without surrender to divine authority feeds the wretchedness of the unregenerate heart.. Enthusiastic converts to this new gospel believe their behavior has no relationship to their spiritual status – even if they continue wantonly in the grossest kinds of sin and expressions of human depravity.[185]

In the same context he adds,

> If you think Paul's doctrine of justification by faith makes it possible for people to lay hold of Christ without letting go of sin, consider…1 Cor 6:9-11…For Paul, perseverance in the faith is essential evidence that faith is real. If a person ultimately and finally falls away from the faith, it proves that that person never really was redeemed to begin with.[186]

In these statements, MacArthur reflects an abandonment of the positional interpretation of *the unrighteous,* in favor of such an extreme *practical* view that he concludes that if someone does not let go of their sin, they were never redeemed in the first place. In addition to showing disregard for stages of growth and progressive sanctification in the believer's life, MacArthur

---

[185] John MacArthur, *The Gospel According to Jesus, Revised and Expanded* (Grand Rapids, MI: Zondervan, 1994), xxi.
[186] Ibid., 249-250.

unabashedly equates discipleship and positional salvation.[187] At that point he has conflated positional and practical (or progressive) salvation.

He illustrates this further when he asserts, "A predilection for such sins reflects an unregenerate heart."[188] In that statement MacArthur seems to disregard the fact that the Corinthians (whom Paul acknowledged were believers in 1:2) were still heavily involved in some of these sins. Paul was writing to challenge the Corinthians to growth and maturity – exactly as MacArthur observed in 1975.

Conclusion

John MacArthur's embracing of the theological hermeneutic over and against the literal grammatical historical hermeneutic has been a driving force behind the development of Lordship salvation, and consequently, of one of the greatest soteriological controversies of our time. That theological hermeneutic is applied generously in Covenant theology, and is foundational in the derivation of such doctrines as limited atonement and replacement theology. (Perhaps this is one reason MacArthur self identifies as a "leaky dispensationalist," as he holds to one and flirts with the other.)

Until we address with finality the issue of consistency in our own hermeneutic methodology, we will fail to recognize that the roots of our soteriological crisis are indeed hermeneutical, and we will continue to be embroiled in controversial issues without any means of resolution. Our challenge is to maintain

---

[187] John MacArthur, *The Gospel According to Jesus, Revised and Expanded* (Grand Rapids, MI: Zondervan, 1994), 35-36, 221.
[188] John MacArthur, *Faith Works: The Gospel According to the Apostles* (Dallas, TX: Word, 1993), 127.

humility and consistency in how we handle the word of God. Our proof texting needs to end, and our exegesis needs to be better grounded in the literal grammatical historical hermeneutic.

14

PRIORITY OF HERMENEUTICS AND THEOLOGICAL METHOD IN METAPHYSICS:
THE DISTINCTION BETWEEN ISRAEL AND THE CHURCH

Charles Ryrie identifies the distinction between Israel and the church as the first component of dispensationalism's tripartite *sine qua non*,[189] and observes that the distinction is "probably the most basic theological test of whether or not a person is a dispensationalist, and...undoubtedly the most practical and conclusive."[190] In light of Ryrie's definitive claim, this paper evaluates five foundational methodological and hermeneutical components of that distinction: (1) authorial intention, (2) progress of revelation, (3) historical context, (4) contextual usage of the term *ekklesia*, and ultimately, (5) literal grammatical historical hermeneutics. The purpose here is to answer five pressing and sometimes overlapping questions:

(1) Did God intend to communicate a distinction?
(2) Does development in the narrative of Scripture corroborate the distinction?

---

[189] Charles C. Ryrie, *Dispensationalism, Revised and Expanded* (Chicago, IL: Moody Press, 1995), 33.
[190] Ibid.

(3) Does the Abrahamic Covenant anticipate the distinction?
(4) Do occurrences of the term *ekklesia* allow for the distinction?
(5) Does a normative reading of the text substantiate the distinction?

If these questions can be answered in the affirmative, then this would constitute strong exegetical evidence that the Bible indeed distinguishes between Israel and the church to the extent that dispensationalism suggests.

Did God Intend to Communicate a Distinction?

If it is true that when we discover what the author intended to communicate we discover the meaning of the communication, then discovering the author's intention in writing must be the primary task of the exegete. When Peter explained the method of revelation (the Holy Spirit moved men who spoke from God, 2 Pet 1:21), he made it clear that while God utilized human writers, God Himself is the ultimate author. Paul asserts that Scripture is God-breathed,[191] and consequently, Philip Payne observes well that because God is the ultimate author of Scripture, "it is His intention alone that exhaustively determines its meaning."[192] That God revealed Himself in this way indicates that God considered the Biblical languages as adequate vehicles to convey His intended meaning in written form. Consequently, if we would understand His

---

[191] 2 Tim 3:16.
[192] Philip Payne, "The Fallacy of Equating Meaning with the Human Author's Intention" in *Journal of the Evangelical Theological Society*, 1977: 243.

intended meaning, we must understand it *from what is written*. Because the Scriptures are useful, ultimately for the equipping of believers,[193] it is evident that they are written in such a way as to be understood.

In assessing the accessibility to the interpreter of the author's intent, E.D Hirsch at first distinguishes between meaning and significance,[194] he later seems even to discount distinction between the two elements, suggesting that "the present of the listener will come after the present of the speaker,"[195] and consequently, meaning is not entirely fixed at the moment of the speech act. In contradistinction to Hirsch's later view of the non-fixity of authorial intent reflected in meaning, we work here from the premise that there is a fixed distinction between meaning (correct interpretation) and significance (application), and that there is a distinction between primary application (the significance of the text for the original audience) and secondary application (the significance of the text for later audiences).[196] Thus the author's intent *is accessible to us in a fixed and certain way, through – and only through – proper handling of the text itself.*

In the case of the theological outcome of distinguishing between Israel and the church we examine a sampling of passages, *in which God is not only the ultimate Author, but is also the One speaking in the first person*. In doing so we consider

---

[193] 2 Tim 3:17.
[194] E.D. Hirsch Jr., *Validity in Interpretation* (London, UK: Yale University Press, 1967), 1.
[195] E.D. Hirsch, Jr., "Meaning and Significance Revisited," *Critical Inquiry* 11 (1984), 206.
[196] Christopher Cone, *Prolegomena on Biblical Hermeneutics and Method*, 2nd Edition (Fort Worth, TX: Tyndale Seminary Press, 2012), 261-262.

whether God intended in those passages to communicate a partial or complete distinction between Israel and the church, or whether He intended to communicate that there is no distinction between the two. It is notable that a non-fixed approach to meaning leads more comfortably to concluding in favor of a continuity between Israel and the church, whereas a fixed approach leads necessarily to a conclusion that the two entities are indeed distinct.

Genesis 12:2-3

God's initial promise to Abram includes seven propositions:

(1) And I will make you a great people or nation
(2) And I will bless you
(3) And I will make your name great
(4) And you will become a blessing
(5) And I will bless the one who blesses you
(6) And the one cursing you I will curse
(7) And they will be blessed in you all families of the earth.

The first six of these are all directly related to Abram, his descendants, or those who relate properly or improperly to him and his descendants. But the seventh proposition is set apart, as it promises a blessing also through Abram for families not connected to Abram. Notice the inclusion here of five distinct people(s) identified in these seven propositions: (1) Abram (2) his descendants (implicit by the process of becoming a great nation), (3) the one who blesses Abram, (4) the one who curses Abram, and (5) all families. Of these five, there are three immediately discernible and distinct groups. We recognize a clear connection between Abram and his descendants, as they will comprise a single great people, and thus an ethnicity.[197] There is no ethnic prerequisite for membership in the ranks of those who bless or curse, as they are described here only by their actions toward Abram. All the families of the earth are yet a third group, but they are distinguished from Abram (and his descendants) by ethnicity: this group is blessed in Abram, but is not Abram. So of the five specific entities involved in the seven propositions, there are three distinct groups of people, and two of those are distinguished by their ethnicity: Abram and his great nation, and all the families of the earth. While it is reasonable that all families[198] might include those descended from Abram, it is also evident that the great nation stemming from Abram would not include all families. While there may be some overlap, there is still ethnic distinction (in other words, all families include Abram's great nation, but Abram's great nation does not include all families). It seems clear enough that God intended to distinguish Abram's descendants as a great nation, from other families and peoples.

Exodus 8:23

God distinguishes between "My people,"[199] Israel and "your people,"[200] Egypt. In Exodus 3:6 God acknowledges that Israel is the nation descended from Abraham, thus more than four hundred years later, God is still maintaining the ethnic distinction introduced in His initial promise to Abram.

---

[197] Heb., *goy.*
[198] Heb., *qal meshpachot.*
[199] Heb., *ami.*
[200] Heb., *amaka.*

1 Samuel 9:16

God distinguishes between "My people," Israel, and the Philistines. Four hundred years after the Exodus, and eight hundred years after God's initial promise to Abram, God specifically continues the ethnic distinction.

Isaiah 19:25

In this remarkable context, God refers to Egypt as "My people,"[201] and yet maintains the ethnic distinctions between Egypt, Assyria, and Israel. God will judge Egypt, but will then heal the nation, allowing Egypt to worship God along with Assyria and Israel. The ethnic distinctiveness remains, yet other nations, besides Israel are blessed. The prophecy of Egypt's blessing reveals an important aspect of God's intention: *He will have other people besides Israel, and yet He intends no dissolution of ethnic distinctions.*

Jeremiah 7:12, 31:31-33

Around 600 B.C., more than twelve hundred years after God's initial promise to Abram, and His initial distinguishing based on ethnicity, God reminds Israel of the continuing distinction. Israel remains God's people. In fact, thirty-eight times in Jeremiah, God calls Israel "My people," including 31:33, which describes God's future intended blessing for "the house of Israel." Two verses earlier God even acknowledges the geographical and political distinction between Israel and Judah, noting that He will make a covenant with both houses, and that covenant will result in a reuniting of two houses into one, as it

---

[201] Heb., *ami*.

was before the division of Israel as a judgment on Solomon for his sin.[202]

Ezekiel 13:9

God makes an important distinction here, announcing that the false prophets who have led Israel astray will not be counted as part of Israel. It becomes evident that God intends that not all who are descended of Israel will be counted as Israel, despite their ethnicity, yet He still maintains Israel's ethnic distinctness as "My people." Thirty times in Ezekiel, God refers to Israel as "My people," including in the contexts of prophesies to be fulfilled in the distant future (such as in chapters 36-46). In all instances, God maintains the ethnic distinctiveness for Israel.

Hosea 1:9-10, 2:23, 6:11

For a time God will say to Israel[203] that they are not His people,[204] but in that place later it will be said that they are sons of God,[205] and they will in the future again be called "My people."[206]

Zephaniah 2:9

God describes future judgment of Moab at the hands of a remnant and remainder of His people. This is a reiteration of an earlier revealed idea that not all who are physically descended from Israel will participate in its prophetic future,[207] yet those

---

[202] 1 Kin 11:9-13.
[203] 1:10a.
[204] 1:10b.
[205] 1:10c, as in Is 64:8.
[206] 2:23, 6:11, etc.
[207] E.g., Ezek 13:9.

who are counted as the remnant and remainder of Israel are ethnic Israel.

Matthew 2:6

Referring to the birthplace of the Messiah, Matthew quotes God's prophecy,[208] in Micah 5:2. This prophecy is different from others considered in this context, as technically Micah is speaking in the first person and God is referenced in the third person, I mention this passage simply to show the Messianic expectation – the understanding of what God intended – was that Israel's distinct status as "My people" would be maintained even during the rule of the Messiah.

Romans 9:25-26

To this point, the distinction between Israel and other ethnicities has been perfectly clear in God's communication. Paul's employment here of Hosea 1:10 and 2:23 represents a potentially pivotal moment – both for the distinctiveness of Israel, and for our understanding of authorial intention.

It is evident from Hosea 1:10 that God is referring to Israel as not being His people (Israel is the "them" to whom it was said "You are not My people."), yet Paul cites the verse in a context[209] that could be understood as supporting that Gentiles are called as vessels of mercy[210] *based on* Hosea 1:10 and 2:23. This understanding may seem to legitimize, for example, Hirsch's idea that meaning is not entirely fixed at the moment of the speech act. God speaks to Hosea referring to Israel, but does Paul change the meaning of the Hosea passages? It would

---

[208] Mic 1:1.
[209] Rom 9:23-26.
[210] 9:23-24.

seem that Hirsch's earlier view is better supported by Romans 9:25-26 than his later view. Paul *does not change the meaning* of the Hosea passages to say that they speak of Gentile salvation, rather he *applies the passage* in such a way as to show that God can indeed designate someone who was not formerly His people as someone who is now His people. This is consistent with what we observe of God's revealed intentions in Isaiah 19:25 – that He will in fact designate those who were not His people as now being His people. As Hirsch initially maintained – and as we maintain here, there is a vital difference between meaning (interpretation) and significance (application). Further, regardless of whether or not God designates Gentiles as His people (and He does), there is no impact on the ethnical distinction God continues to maintain between Israel and non-Jews.

2 Corinthians 6:16-18

Paul's allusion to several OT passages here help to confirm that his usage of the Hosea passages in Romans 9:25-26 does not represent a change in meaning. In verse 16, Paul says that we,[211] as believers in Christ, are collectively a[212] temple of God.

In each of the OT passages similar to Paul's statement,[213] the antecedent of the pronoun *them* is Israel. Paul does not reshape the meaning of the passage, but rather uses the passage to illustrate that a temple of God[214] ought to be separate from

---

[211] He and the primarily Gentile Corinthians.
[212] There is no definite article before *temple*.
[213] Ex 25:8, 29:45-46, Lev 26:12, and Jer 31:1.
[214] 2 Cor 6:16.

idols.²¹⁵ By this reference Paul provides an answer to the rhetorical question of 6:16.²¹⁶ Just as Israel was a temple of God, and the people were expected to be holy, so the church is a temple of God, and should be holy.

Importantly, there is nothing here to indicate that God intends for us to understand that Israel and the church are *the same temple*. The absence of the definite article preceding each instance of *temple*²¹⁷ helps to confirm what this context implies – that there is more than one temple of God.

Hebrews 8:10

Simply put, this context quotes the New Covenant of Jeremiah 31, to illustrate that Christ's ministry is simply better,²¹⁸ and thus to provide another evidence that *He is better*. There is no direct application of the New Covenant to the church, and the original ethnicity-distinctive language is left intact, as 8:10 restates that Israel will be His people. This quotation of the New Covenant is significant for a number of reasons, one of which is that even two thousand years after God's initial promise to Abram, there was an expectation on the part of the writer of Hebrews that God intended to maintain the distinction between Israel and other nations in fulfilling the New Covenant literally with Israel, and not with other nations.

---

²¹⁵ 6:17.
²¹⁶ What agreement has a [no definite article] temple of God with idols?
²¹⁷ Gr., *naos*.
²¹⁸ 8:6.

Revelation 18:4

This passage includes a call, seemingly from God, for "My people"[219] to come out of Babylon the great. It is not explicit in the immediate context who is the intended referent of "My people." As it has been established previously in Scripture that God does call other peoples besides Israel "My people,"[220] so Revelation 18:4 does not provide any information that would either persuade or dissuade regarding whether or not there is a continuing distinction between Israel and the Church. Working from the trajectory that earlier passages set, it appears that this is a call to believing Jews to come out of Babylon the great, but this is admittedly more a theological rather than exegetical conclusion in this case.

Conclusion

These passages, most of which record God speaking directly in the first person, demonstrate that He intended to communicate a longstanding and future-looking distinction between ethnic Israel and other nations – including peoples who are blessed,[221] and even called people of God.[222] He communicates that not all of ethnic Israel will be counted as Israel,[223] yet those who will be blessed *as Israel* will be ethnically Jewish.[224]

---

[219] Gr., *ho laos mou*.
[220] Is. 19:25.
[221] Gen 12:3.
[222] Is 19:25.
[223] Ezek 13:9.
[224] Jer 31:31, Zeph 2:9.

Does Development in the Narrative Corroborate the Distinction?

In Reformed perspective, the "church has existed from the beginning of the world, and will last until the end..."[225] That Belgic statement indicates an understanding of Biblical chronology that necessitates the non-distinction of Israel and the church. Keith Mathison explains well the basic Covenantalist view that the church and true Israel are not really distinct at all. Mathison observes that,

> The church is distinct from national Israel, just as the true Israel in the Old Testament was distinct from national Israel even while being part of national Israel. The remnant group was part of the whole but could also be distinguished from the whole by its faith.[226]

He adds a key point that,

> [I]f we are talking about true Israel, there really is no distinction. The true Israel of the Old Testament became the nucleus of the true church on the day of Pentecost...It means that when true Israel was baptized by the Spirit on the day of Pentecost, true Israel became the New Testament church.[227]

---

[225] The Belgic Confession, Article 27, (1561), viewed at http://www.crcna.org/welcome/beliefs/confessions/belgic-confession.
[226] Keith Mathison, "The Church and Israel in the New Testament," Ligionier Ministries, viewed at http://www.ligonier.org/learn/articles/the-church-and-israel-in-the-new-testament/.
[227] Ibid.

The Baptism of the Holy Spirit and The Timing of the Church's Genesis

While it is fair to say that at Pentecost, at least some of the people in Jerusalem who were "true Israel" in the Romans 9:6 sense became the New Testament church – as the church was initially entirely Jewish, it is not accurate or logically valid to therefore conclude that the New Testament church *is* true Israel. One problem with that view is that there were many believers who were "true Israel" who were not in Jerusalem at Pentecost, and who did not become part of the church until later,[228] consequently, *true Israel*, as a single entity, was not baptized by the Spirit on the day of Pentecost, though some individual members of true Israel were.

In the progress of revelation, the baptism of the Holy Spirit is the crucial point in the formation of the church. 1 Corinthians 12:13 describes how "we" all were baptized by one Spirit into the body of Christ. When the baptism of the Holy Spirit is first introduced in Scripture, John the Baptist distinguishes between the present and future to announce that while he was baptizing,[229] Jesus would baptize with the Holy Spirit.[230] John introduces a clear anticipation that there would be a future baptism accomplished by Jesus in which the Holy Spirit would be the baptizing agent.

While John's Gospel records that Jesus baptized disciples early in His earthly ministry, it is also careful to note that Jesus Himself wasn't doing the baptizing.[231] Neither Matthew, Mark,

---

[228] E.g., Apollos in Acts 18:24-26, and the disciples of John in 19:1-7, compare with 1 Cor 12:13.
[229] Gr., *baptizo*, present active indicative.
[230] Gr., *baptisei*, future active indicative.
[231] Jn 3:22, 4:1-2.

nor Luke record that Jesus actually did any baptizing. All three agree in identifying the initial promise that He would baptize with the Spirit,[232] and none of the three include in their Gospels any discussion of the fulfillment of that prediction. Meanwhile, in the upper room, Jesus preannounced the coming of the Holy Spirit in a manner distinct from His previous ministries: in the future He would be given,[233] sent by Father and Son[234] to be with the disciples forever,[235] and He would testify about Christ.[236] In Acts 1:4 Jesus commands the disciples to wait in Jerusalem for the baptism of the Holy Spirit, whom would come "not many days from now." Consistently, the Gospel writers anticipate the baptism to be in the future, and Luke's Acts account records Christ as specifying that the prophecy would be fulfilled very quickly.

Obviously, the baptism of the Holy Spirit was a new development, and as of Acts 1 *it had not yet happened.* The fulfillment began in Acts 2 with the coming of the Spirit. In Acts 11:15-17, Peter directly connects the event at Pentecost and the Gentiles' receiving of the Holy Spirit with Jesus' prophecy. Paul later describes the baptism of the Holy Spirit as the means of entrance for believers[237] into the church as the body of Christ.[238] For those at Jerusalem who were not initially baptized by the Holy Spirit at Pentecost in Acts 2:1-5, they were told to repent and they would be forgiven and receive the gift of the Holy

---

[232] Mt 3:11, Mk 1:8, Lk 3:16.
[233] Gr., *dosei*, future active indicative.
[234] Jn 15:26.
[235] Jn 14:16.
[236] Jn 15:26.
[237] 1 Cor 12:12-13.
[238] Rom 12:4-5; 1 Cor 10:16, 12:12-27; Eph 1:23, 3:6, 4:4, 12-16, 5:23-30, Col 1:24, 2:19, 3:15.

Spirit.[239] By the time Paul wrote 1 Corinthians 12:12-13, the baptism of the Holy Spirit was normative for all believers.

Abraham's Descendants and the Identity of True Israel Revealed

A second problem is that to assert true Israel is the church and therefore the church is true Israel commits the logical fallacy of affirming the consequent.[240] In this context Mathison does not quite go that far, but he does assert that the church, along with true Israel forms "the one people of God."[241] However, Martin Luther does go as far as to say that "All Gentiles who are Christians are the true Israelites and new Jews, born of Christ, the noblest Jew."[242] John Calvin, likewise, extends as far as to consider Gentiles as part of true Israel, saying, "The salvation of the whole Israel of God, which must be drawn from both [Jews and Gentiles]..."[243]

A consequence of this logical challenge in considering the church as true Israel is the necessary assertion that believing Gentiles somehow gain a spiritual ethnicity, yet believing Jews maintain their ethnicity. Thomas Schreiner argues, for example,

---

[239] Repent is the only condition here for forgiveness and receiving the Holy Spirit, as the Gr., *metanoesate* is aorist active imperative, second person plural, the two resulting conditions are also in the second person plural, while the baptism imperative, Gr., *baptistheto*, is in third person singular, a separate clause. Acts 10:47 confirms that water baptism was done for people who had already received the Holy Spirit.
[240] Represented formally as: If P then Q. Q. Therefore P.
[241] Mathison, "The Church and Israel in the New Testament."
[242] Martin Luther, *Luther's Works* (Fortress Press, Concordia, Faithlife, 1900-1986), 35:288
[243] John Calvin, *The Epistles of Paul the Apostle to the Romans and to the Thessalonians*, ed. D.W. Torrance and T.F. Torrance, trans. R. Mackenzie (Grand Rapids, MI: Eerdmans, 1961), 255.

that because Paul refers in Philippians 3:3 to spiritual circumcision and then in 3:5 to physical circumcision, that it is not impossible that Paul could view there as being both a physical and spiritual Israel.[244] Schreiner cites in support of this possibility Galatians 3:29 and 6:16, focusing on the church's identification as the seed of Abraham (3:29), and states that "By NT times to be a son of Abraham or the seed of Abraham was equivalent to being a Jew."[245]

But in this Schreiner moves from possibility to actuality without sufficient support. It is a critical omission that Schreiner does not in this context acknowledge the Romans 4 identifications of three distinct people groups as the seed or children of Abraham: (1) the fleshly father of Israel – Jews in general,[246] (2) the father of those who have faith but are not Israelite according to the flesh – believing Gentiles,[247] and (3) the father of those who are both of faith and also of Israel according to the flesh – believing Jews.[248] It is clear especially from Romans 4:11 that Paul does not view being a descendant of Abraham as equivalent to being Jewish, as he clearly distinguishes between the two groups in that context. While Schreiner argues for the church as new Israel on grounds that Paul taught that believing Gentiles were Jewish equivalents, the narrative development – especially in Romans 4 – regarding the seed of Abraham contradicts the idea that being a child of Abraham meant being Jewish.

---

[244] Thomas Schreiner, "The Church as the New Israel and the Future of Ethnic Israel in Paul" in *Studia Biblica et Theologica*, 13 (1983): 19-20.
[245] Ibid., 20.
[246] 4:1.
[247] 4:11.
[248] 4:12.

In Schreiner's commentary on Romans, it seems Schreiner recognizes that being the seed of Abraham is not equivalent with being Jewish, as he says,

> Abraham was always intended to be the father of all peoples (4:9-16). The promise cannot be restricted to the Jewish people, for the oath made was always intended to embrace the entire world.[249]

He adds,

> ...grace secures the promise to all Abraham's children (16c), that is, both Jew and Gentiles who have faith, since Abraham is the father of both (16d).[250]

In this understanding, it would seem the only way possible for all the seed of Abraham to be Jews, and at the same time Abraham to be the father of Jews, believing Jews, and believing Gentiles is *if every believing Gentile becomes a spiritual Jew, and if unbelieving Jews were not counted as Jews at all.*

Schreiner further complicates the passage, asserting Paul to be teaching that "Abraham is the father only of Jews who have faith. Circumcision is insufficient to belong to the people of God."[251] Schreiner acknowledges an exegetical challenge with this view:

---

[249] Thomas Schreiner, *Romans: Baker Exegetical Commentary on the New Testament* (Grand Rapids, MI, 1998), 177.
[250] Ibid., 223.
[251] Ibid., 226.

> [S]ince a previous use of τοῖς is found after περιτομῆς, the τοῖς...τοῖς construction suggests that two sets of people are included in verse 12. If the repetition of τοῖς designates two distinct groups of people, then those who are circumcised would be one set of Abraham's children, and those who walk in faith would be another set.[252]

It is interesting that in order to achieve a reading that supports the spiritual Jew view, Schreiner concludes,

> The double τοῖς construction is difficult, but the syntax is a bit awkward here in any case, and Paul did not always abide by the grammatical rules of his day.[253]

Remarkably, Schreiner dismisses the simplest grammatical understanding, apparently because the resulting progress of Paul's narrative would counter the Reformed theological position. Ultimately, Schreiner is forced to deny that unbelieving Jews are descended at all from Abraham, in order to support that believing Gentiles are spiritual Jews. Schreiner's approach to the ethnicity of believing Gentiles and unbelieving Jews supports a continuity between Israel and the church, and is consistent with the broader Reformed idea that the church ultimately began with Adam and is comprised of all believers throughout history.

Conclusion

In contrast to Reformed view that the church began with the first believer, the chronological progress of revelation

---

[252] Ibid.
[253] Ibid.

identifies two major narrative themes that support a standing chronological distinction between Israel and the church. First, the baptism by the Holy Spirit as prophesied by Christ is not fulfilled until the early development of the book of Acts, and is reckoned to be the exclusive marker of entrance into the church. Second, even after the baptism prophecy is fulfilled, Israel maintains its ethnic identity – as do the other groups identified as descendants of Abraham (including unbelieving Jews). These two – along with the simple fact that while Israel existed as a distinct ethnic entity before and after, the *ekklesia* was predicted as still yet future when Christ introduced it[254] – show a marked distinction between Israel and the church.

Does the Abrahamic Covenant Anticipate the Distinction?

Genesis 15 describes the covenant God made with Abraham,[255] specifically promising an heir and innumerable descendants,[256] a four-hundred year slavery and return of his descendants,[257] and an expansive land in which to dwell.[258] The covenant reiterates and expands aspects of God's earlier promise to Abraham in Genesis 12, a promise which includes seven propositions:

(1) And I will make you a great people or nation
(2) And I will bless you
(3) And I will make your name great
(4) And you will become a blessing

---

[254] Mt 16:18.
[255] 15:18.
[256] 15:4-5.
[257] 15:13-16.
[258] 15:18-21.

(5) And I will bless the one who blesses you
(6) And the one cursing you I will curse
(7) And they will be blessed in you all families of the earth.

The first four propositions pertain to Abraham's descendants becoming a great and blessed nation, the next two promise blessing or curse to those who treat Abraham's descendants well or poorly, and the seventh guarantees blessing through Abraham for all the families of the earth. As was discussed earlier, God's clear intention is to communicate an ethnic discontinuity between the descendants of Abraham and other families of the earth who will be blessed through Abraham. The task at hand in this section is to consider how, if at all, the Abrahamic covenant anticipates specifically a substantive distinction between Israel and the church.

In consideration of God's promise to make Abraham's descendants a great and blessed nation, God adds specificity through the establishing of further covenants to three components prerequisite for national elements: a land, a people, and a government. The land elements are first considered in Genesis 12:1, as God directs Abram "to the land which I will show you." That land is further delineated in Genesis 15, and notably so by ethnic divisions rather than simply geographical ones. There were discernible geographical markers, such as the peoples' placement in relation to two key rivers, but the ethnic associations were at least equally prominent. To the (singular) seed of Abraham the land is given.

Israel's future tenure in that land is outlined in the covenant God made with Israel at Moab.[259] After a period of judgment, God would gather Israel out from the peoples where they would have been scattered. This promise means nothing if it does not mean that Israel would remain ethnically distinct. It is significant that God employs the phrase *from among the peoples*[260] to describe Israel's return from scattering in a locative sense. The land in this context is again reckoned by ethnic associations rather than strictly geographic markers. Further, God adds that He would bring Israel back, referring to the nation not in the singular, but in the second person plural. It would not simply be the nation of Israel that would possess the land, it would be *individual Israelites*.

Finally, the land will be possessed by a spiritually regenerated and yet ethnically identifiable Israel,[261] but the peoples (nations) will stream to it, in pilgrimage.[262] There is no indication whatsoever in the promises of any non-Israelite *possession* of the land. The specific land aspects stemming from the Abrahamic Covenant anticipate that the promises will be fulfilled both nationally and individually by ethnic Israelites, as distinct from the nations who will enjoy blessings of God's presence there. Within the context of these land blessings, it is evident that there is anticipated a continuous distinction between Israel and non-Israelite peoples.

The second consideration in order for the Abrahamic Covenant to be fulfilled is a government or kingdom element.

---

[259] Deut 29:1ff. This covenant is often referred to as the Palestinian Covenant, though I prefer the term, the Land Covenant.
[260] Heb., *mikal–haamim*.
[261] Ezek 37:11-14.
[262] Is 2:3.

Genesis 49:1 and 10 predict that Judah will be the royal tribe. God made a covenant[263] in 2 Samuel 7:8-17 with David that expanded on that prophecy, assuring David of (1) a great name, (2) a place for Israel, (3) rest from enemies, (4) a house for David, (5) a descendant after David who would build a house for God, and (6) the establishment of the throne of his kingdom forever. That particular descendant's (Solomon's) kingdom would not be forever, but the throne of his kingdom would be. God expands this Davidic Covenant further, explaining in Jeremiah 33:14-22 that His covenant with David is unbreakable, that a righteous Branch of David would spring forth, His rule would be characterized by justice and righteousness, and in it Judah and Jerusalem would dwell in safety. The first to Jesus in the NT identifies Him as the Son of David, and the last time He identifies Himself by name He refers to Himself as the root and descendant of David.[264]

Revelation 20 describes the beginning of the Messianic rule, as described in Isaiah 9:6-7,

> There will be no end to the increase of His government or of peace, on the throne of David and over His kingdom, to uphold it and establish it with justice and righteousness from then on and forevermore. The zeal of the Lord of hosts will accomplish this.

The Messiah's rule will be on David's throne – in Jerusalem, and over David's kingdom – the ethnic house of Israel.

The final issue that must be resolved in order to have a blessed nation is the *people* aspect of the Abrahamic Covenant,

---

[263] Ps 89:3.
[264] Mt 1:1 and Rev 22:16.

in order to provide a way for an eternal people, by resolving the sin problem that would keep the covenant people from being able to receive the blessings of the covenants eternally. This *people* element of the Abrahamic Covenant is first discussed in the context of the conditional Mosaic Covenant, introduced in Exodus 19:5, "if you will indeed obey My voice and keep My covenant, then you shall be My own possession among the peoples..." This covenant with Israel through Moses was conditioned upon Israel's obedience, and provided means where (at least) certain sins could be forgiven through the shedding of animal blood.[265] But as the Law unfolded, it became evident that even though Israel would be able to understand the requirements God had for the nation,[266] Israel would be incapable of obeying the covenant, and would reap the requisite judgment.[267] Further, it is evident that the Law was never intended to deal decisively with Israel's sin issue.[268] Instead, the Law served to exacerbate the sin problem[269] and expose it, in order to demonstrate the need for a Redeemer.[270]

In contrast to the Mosaic Covenant, which was conditional, God would later establish the New Covenant, which would be premised on a physical restoration of the people of Israel,[271] and a heightened individual rather than national responsibility.[272] The covenant would be expressly with the house of Israel and the house of Judah – a clear and delineated

---

[265] E.g., Lev 4:14-20, 26, 31, 35; 5:10, 13,16,18, etc.
[266] Deut 30:11-14.
[267] Deut 30:1 / c.f., Deut 15:4-5 and 15:11.
[268] Ps 40:6-8, Gal 3:17-18, Heb 10:4-6.
[269] Rom 3:19, 4:15, 5:20, 7:8.
[270] Gal 3:23-25.
[271] Jer 31:27-28, 31:38-40.
[272] Jer 31:29-30.

ethnic group,²⁷³ and it would differ from the former Mosaic Covenant.²⁷⁴ The covenant involved an internal or spiritual restoration, accompanying the physical and national one, as He would write His law on their heart, and He would be their God and they would be His people.²⁷⁵ Further, every individual of the Israel and Judah would know Him, and would be forgiven their sins.²⁷⁶ God affirms the certainty of the covenant, and reiterates that it would be kept with the offspring of Israel.²⁷⁷ This New Covenant resolves the sin problem for Israel once and for all, providing for forgiveness of sin and a right relationship to God.

The New Covenant is mentioned seven times in the NT. Luke 22:20 records Jesus' statement that the cup was the New Covenant in His blood. In 1 Corinthians 11:25 Paul quotes Jesus' statement, as recorded by Luke, and identifies in v. 26 the application for the church is to proclaim Jesus' death until He comes. In these passages, neither Jesus nor Paul makes direct reference to the New Covenant being applied to the church. Paul later describes in 2 Corinthians 3:6 that "we are servants of a new covenant." In the immediate context, the antecedent of the pronoun *we* is not believers, nor the Corinthians,²⁷⁸ but is rather Paul, Silvanus, and Timothy.²⁷⁹ Thus the passage is not a reference to the church in general as serving the New Covenant, but rather perhaps Paul magnifying His service to the Gentiles as helping to facilitate the future fulfillment of the New

---

[273] Jer 31:31.
[274] Jer 31:32.
[275] Jer 31:33.
[276] Jer 31:34.
[277] Jer 35:37.
[278] Paul refers to the Corinthians as "you," for example, in 3:2,3 and 4:12.
[279] 2 Cor 1:19.

Covenant, by drawing the Jews to jealousy for their Messiah.[280] The other four references to the New Covenant appear in Hebrews 8:8,13, 9:15, and 12:24, as the New Covenant is identified as a better mediatorship than that of Moses, thus demonstrating the superiority of the Jesus over Moses. The writer's purpose in this section of Hebrews is not to apply the covenant to the church, but to demonstrate that His blood that was poured out to ratify the New Covenant also was poured out to pay for the sins of all. It is through the better hope – the blood of Christ, in contrast to the blood of goats and bulls – that we draw near to God.[281] None of these passages draws any conclusion that the New Covenant is applied to the church, nor is such a conclusion either exegetically or theologically necessary.[282]

The final component of the Abrahamic Covenant is ethnically universal blessing through the Seed of Abraham, as prophesied in Genesis 12:3b. In Galatians 3:8 Paul describes this passage as a prophetic presentation of the gospel, that God would save the Gentiles by faith. This promise is consistent with the people delineated in Romans 4:11, as those who believe without being circumcised – or believing Gentiles. This salvation is paid for by the Messiah, the seed of Eve, and the seed of Abraham as anticipated in the *protevangelium* of Genesis 3:15, and in God's Genesis 22:13 substitutionary provision of the ram as a sacrifice.

---

[280] Rom 11:12-14.
[281] Heb 7:19, 9:21-28.
[282] For more detail on this assertion, please see Christopher Cone, "The Hermeneutic Ramifications of Applying the New Covenant to the Church" in *An Introduction to the New Covenant*, gen. ed., Christopher Cone (Fort Worth, TX, Tyndale Seminary Press: 2013), 79-108.

Conclusion

The Abrahamic Covenant provides the skeletal system for God's plan of the ages, as He structures His promises after the initial statement of that covenant in such a way as to be directly traceable to the Abrahamic Covenant – the Land Covenant to provide a place for the blessed nation, the Davidic Covenant to provide for its government and King, the New Covenant in order to provide for its people, the Mosaic Covenant to offer a conditional contrast to demonstrate the universality of sin and need for a Redeemer in anticipation of the New Covenant, and finally, the blessing of the Gentiles also through the Seed of Abraham. Nowhere in these covenants is there any blurring of ethnic distinctions, neither in their promising nor in their fulfilling. God's promises are rooted in ethnic distinctions, and there is nothing in the Abrahamic Covenant nor in the covenants following that would suggest a future undoing of ethnic distinctions in their future fulfillments. Consequently, the Abrahamic Covenant and the covenants that follow support the distinction between those who are descended of Abraham and to whom pertain the great nation promises and those who are ethnically not descended from Abraham, yet are his children through faith, and to whom are promised blessing through Abraham's Seed.

Do Occurrences of the Term *Ekklesia* Allow for the Distinction?

The purpose of this analysis is to determine whether the use of the term *ekklesia* allows for the distinction between Israel and the church, and whether there are *any* instances in which the *ekklesia* is synonymous with Israel. If there be any instances of the latter, then it might be reasonable to understand passages not identifying the *ekklesia* with Israel in light of those passages that do.

In examination of all instances in the Greek NT[283] of forms of the term *ekklesia*, we consider four possible categorizations of each. The category identified as *C* refers distinctly to the church universal or its local membership. The category *O* refers to an assembly distinct from the church or Israel. In the category labeled *NE*, the referent is not specifically evident. And in the category *I*, the referent is primarily Israel – either geographical, ethnic, or spiritual.

References directly to the church universal or its local membership: (Total C = 69)

Mt 16:18 – This first reference is strongly indicative of a distinction between Israel and the church, as Jesus announces that He will build[284] His *ekklesia* on "this rock," whereas He had previously acknowledged that Israel was already established.[285] Category: C.

Mt 18:17 – Immediately following the context of the prophesied new assembly, and immediately followed by a repetition or the authority of Peter and the apostles in this assembly (twice).[286] C

Ac 5:11 – set in Jerusalem, the *ekklesia* is distinguished from all who heard these things. C

---

[283] NA28.
[284] Gr., *oikodomeso*, future indicative.
[285] E.g., Mt 8:10.
[286] Cf., 16:19 and 18:18.

Ac 8:1 – the church was persecuted in Jerusalem, and as a result scattered into Judea and Samaria. Judea and Samaria clearly distinct from the church. C

Ac 8:3 – By entering only some houses and not all, Saul distinguished between the church and Israel. C

Ac 9:31 – The church distinguished from geographical regions, though identified in geographical regions. C

Ac 11:22 – The specific assembly at Jerusalem is distinguished from the rest of Jerusalem. C

Ac 11:26 – The church in the Roman province of Antioch, comprised also of non-Jews, distinguishing it from geographical and ethnic Israel. C

Ac 13:1 – Distinction between the church as a non-geographical entity and its geographical placement, and comprised of some non-Jews. C

Ac 14:23 – Each church (*kat ekklesian*) considered autonomous to some degree, having elders appointed for their leadership. Church is neither geographic nor ethnic, also comprised of some non-Jews. C

Ac 14:27 – The church at Antioch receives a report of God's inclusion of non-Jews. C

Ac 15:3 – Paul and Barnabas sent by the church at Judea through Phoenicia and Samaria to Jerusalem. Church neither geographic nor ethnic. C

Ac 15:4 – Church at Jerusalem, distinct from inhabitants of Jerusalem, including Pharisees. C

Ac 15:41 – Churches, plural, in various geographical areas throughout Syria and Cilicia. C

Ac 16:5 – Churches, plural, in various geographical areas throughout Derbe and Lystra. C

Ac 18:22 – Church geographically distinguished as being local at Caesarea. C

Ac 20:17 – Church at Ephesus has elders, distinct from elders of Israel (as in Ac 6:12). C

Ac 20:28 – Overseers to shepherd the church, but are not seen as having any authoritative role in Israel. Church identified as being purchased with His blood, later identified as "from every tribe and tongue and people and nation (Rev 5:9), and not exclusively ethnic or geographic Israel. C

Rom 16:1 – A local church at Cenchrea. C

Rom 16:4 – Local churches comprised (primarily) of Gentiles. C

Rom 16:5 – A house church among the Gentiles.

Rom 16:16 – Churches (plural) of Christ indicates distinct parts that make up the whole, comprised of both Jew and Gentile. C

Rom 16:23 – Perhaps a house church meeting in Gaius' home? If so, distinctly local, and not connected with Israel. C

1 Cor 1:2 – Church of God at Corinth, comprised largely of Gentiles. C

1 Cor 4:17 – Every church includes churches comprised of both Jew and Gentile. C

1 Cor 7:17 – All the churches include churches comprised of both Jew and Gentile. C

1 Cor 10:32 – Church of God directly distinguished from Jews and Gentiles. Comprised of people from both groups, yet the church is not either of those groups. C

1 Cor 11:16 – The churches of God denotes a plurality of local assemblies, making up the greater whole. C

1 Cor 11:18 – Corinthians coming together as a distinct assembly. C

1 Cor 14:23 – The whole church comes together in a local iteration. C

1 Cor 14:33 – The churches denotes a plurality of local assemblies, making up the greater whole. C

1 Cor 14:34 – The churches denotes a plurality of local assemblies, making up the greater whole. C

1 Cor 16:1 – The churches of Galatia, a large region of Asia Minor, distinct from Israel. C

1 Cor 16:19 – The churches of Asia, distinct from Israel, and the church that met in the house of Aquila and Prisca (two references) C

2 Cor 1:1 – The church of God, located at Corinth and all saints at Achaia. Geographically distinct from Israel. C

2 Cor 8:1 – Churches, plural, of Macedonia. Geographically distinct from Israel. C

2 Cor 8:18 – All the churches, as distinct entities. C

2 Cor 8:19 – By the churches, as distinct entities. C

2 Cor 8:23 – Brethren as messengers of the churches, as distinct entities. C

2 Cor 8:24 – The churches, as distinct entities. C

2 Cor 11:8 – Other churches distinguished from the church at Corinth. C

2 Cor 11:28 – For all the churches, as distinct entities with distinct burdens. C

2 Cor 12:13 – Corinth distinguished from other churches. C

Gal 1:2 – Churches of Galatia as distinct entities. C

Gal 1:22 – Churches of Judea distinguished from churches of Galatia. C

Php 4:15 – Church at Philippi distinguished from other churches. C

Col 4:15 – Distinct church meeting in the house of Nympha. C

Col 4:16 – Distinction drawn between the churches at Colossae and Laeodicea. C

1 Thes 1:1 – Distinct church at Thessalonica. C

1 Thes 2:14 – Churches in Judea distinct from church at Thessalonica. C

2 Thes 1:1 – Church at Thessalonica as distinct entity. C

2 Thes 1:4 – Church at Thessalonica distinctly identifiable among churches of God. C

Philem 2 – Distinct church in Philemon's house. C

1 Jn 3:6 – The church as a finite entity, before whom John testified of Gaius' love. C

1 Jn 3:9 – The church as a finite entity, among whom was Diotrophes. C

Rev 1:4 – Seven distinguishable churches of Asia. C

Rev 1:11 – Seven distinguishable churches of Asia. C

Rev 1:20 – Seven distinguishable churches of Asia (twice). C

Rev 2:1 – Church at Ephesus as distinct entity. C

Rev 2:8 – Church at Smyrna as distinct entity. C

Rev 2:12 – Church at Pergamum as distinct entity. C

Rev 2:18 – Church at Thyatira as distinct entity. C

Rev 2:23 – All the churches as distinct entities. C

Rev 3:1 – Church at Sardis as distinct entity. C

Rev 3:7 – Church at Philadelphia as distinct entity. C

Rev 3:14 – Church at Laodicea as distinct entity. C

Instances in which the referent is specifically an assembly other than the church or Israel: (Total O = 3)

Ac 19:32 – A public gathering of Ephesians, contrasted with the church, and as coming against the church. O

Ac 19:39 – A legal assembly to be convened by the town clerk to determine what was to be done with Alexander and the disciples. O

Ac 19:41 – A public gather of Ephesians. O

Instances in which the referent is not specifically evident in the immediate context: (Total NE = 40)

Ac 12:1 – Nonspecific reference to members of the church. NE

Ac 12:5 – Nonspecific reference to members of the church. NE

Ac 15:22 – Nonspecific reference to members of the church. NE

1 Cor 6:4 – Nonspecific reference to the church. NE

1 Cor 11:22 – Nonspecific reference to the church. NE

1 Cor 12:28 – Nonspecific reference to the church. NE

1 Cor 14:4 – Nonspecific reference to the church. NE

1 Cor 14:5 – Nonspecific reference to the church. NE

1 Cor 14:12 – Nonspecific reference to the church. NE

1 Cor 14:19 – Nonspecific reference to the church. NE

1 Cor 14:28 – Nonspecific reference to the church. NE

1 Cor 14:35 – Nonspecific reference to the church. NE

1 Cor 15:9 – Nonspecific reference to the church of God. NE

Gal 1:13 – Nonspecific reference to the church of God. NE

Eph 1:22 – Nonspecific reference to the church of God. NE

Eph 3:10 – Nonspecific reference to the church of God. NE

Eph 3:21 – Nonspecific reference to the church of God. NE

Eph 5:23 – Nonspecific reference to the church of God. NE

Eph 5:24 – Nonspecific reference to the church of God. NE

Eph 5:25 – Nonspecific reference to the church of God. NE

Eph 5:27 – Nonspecific reference to the church of God. NE

Eph 5:29 – Nonspecific reference to the church of God. NE

Eph 5:32 – Nonspecific reference to the church of God. NE

Php 3:6 – Nonspecific reference to the church of God. NE

Col 1:18 – Nonspecific reference to the church of God. NE

Col 1:24 – Nonspecific reference to the church of God. NE

1 Tim 3:5 – Nonspecific reference to the church of God. NE

1 Tim 3:15 – Nonspecific reference to the church of God. NE

1 Tim 5:16 – Nonspecific reference to the church. NE

Heb 12:23 – Nonspecific reference to the church of the firstborn. NE

Jam 5:14 – Nonspecific reference to the church of God. NE

1 Jn 3:10 – Nonspecific reference to the church. NE

Rev 2:7 – Might be directly referring to seven churches of Asia, but not exegetically necessary. NE

Rev 2:11 – Might be directly referring to seven churches of Asia, but not exegetically necessary. NE

Rev 2:17 – Might be directly referring to seven churches of Asia, but not exegetically necessary. NE

Rev 2:29 – Might be directly referring to seven churches of Asia, but not exegetically necessary. NE

Rev 3:6 – Might be directly referring to seven churches of Asia, but not exegetically necessary. NE

Rev 3:13 – Might be directly referring to seven churches of Asia, but not exegetically necessary. NE

Rev 3:22 – Might be directly referring to seven churches of Asia, but not exegetically necessary. NE

Rev 22:16 – Might be directly referring to seven churches of Asia, but not exegetically necessary. NE

Instances in which the referent of ekklesia is primarily Israel, geographically, ethnically, or spiritually: (Total = 2)

Ac 7:38 – A clear reference to ethnic Israel, not geographic or spiritual.

Heb 2:12 – A quote of Psalm 22:22, referring to the assembly[287] of the Psalmist's brethren, apparently, Israel.

Implications and Conclusion

       In examination of one hundred and fourteen appearances in the Greek NT of forms of the term *ekklesia*, sixty nine instances (labeled *C*) refer distinctly to the church universal or its local membership, three to non-ethnic-specific assemblies in Ephesus (labeled *O*), in forty instances (labeled *NE*) the referent is generally to the church, but not specific with regard to any connection to or disconnection from ethnic Israel, and in two instances (labeled *I*) the referent is ethnic Israel, in recounting ancient historical contexts. Considering that Acts 7:38 and Hebrews 2:12 provide the only specific references to Israel as *ekklesia*, it is notable that both instances simply recount historical events prior to Jesus' prophecy that He would, in the

---

[287] In the LXX, the Gr., *ekklesia* translates the Heb., *qahal*.

future tense, build His *ekklesia* on Himself, as the stone of stumbling and the rock of offense.[288] Consequently, the NT use of the term *ekklesia* provides no support for Israel and the church as interchangeable, but instead provides sixty nine instances of support for the distinctiveness of the church from ethnic or geographical Israel. Further, the term provides no support whatsoever for any concept of the church as spiritual Israel.

Conclusion: A Normative Reading of the Text Substantiates a Complete and Lasting Distinction Between Israel and the Church

In this chapter we have sought to resolve four major questions:

(1) Did God intend to communicate a distinction?
(2) Does development in the narrative of Scripture corroborate the distinction?
(3) Does the Abrahamic Covenant anticipate the distinction?
(4) Do occurrences of the term *ekklesia* allow for the distinction?

In the resolution of these four questions, we settle an ultimate fifth question:

(5) Does a normative reading of the text substantiate the distinction?

---

[288] Is 8:14, 1 Pet 2:4-10.

The answers collectively provide a definitive answer on whether or not an ongoing distinction between Israel and the church is exegetically warranted and theologically appropriate.

First, we discover from a number of key passages which record God as speaking directly in the first person, that God indeed intended to communicate a longstanding and future-looking distinction between ethnic Israel and other nations – including peoples who are blessed, and even called people of God. He communicates that not all of ethnic Israel will be counted as Israel, yet those who will be blessed *as Israel* will be ethnically Jewish.

Second, we encounter in the progress of revelation two prominent themes that support a standing chronological distinction between Israel and the church: (1) the baptism by the Holy Spirit, first prophesied by John, then Christ, then later fulfilled progressively in the book of Acts, as the decisive marker of entrance into the church; and (2) even after the baptism prophecy is fulfilled in Acts, Israel and other groups identified as descendants of Abraham maintains their distinctive ethnic identities. These two themes strongly support the marked distinction between Israel and the church.

Third, the Abrahamic Covenant is the key to understanding the unfolding of God's plan. That covenant and all those that follow are careful not to allow for any blurring of ethnic distinctions, instead being firmly rooted in ethnic distinctions. Consequently, the Abrahamic Covenant and the covenants that follow support the distinction between those who are descended of Abraham and to whom pertain the great nation promises and those who are ethnically not descended from Abraham, yet are his children through faith, and to whom are promised blessing through Abraham's Seed.

Fourth, an examination of the one hundred and fourteen appearances in the Greek NT of forms of the term *ekklesia* provides strong evidence supporting the distinction between Israel and the church, as sixty-nine instances refer directly to the church universal or its local membership, three instances refer to non-ethnic assemblies not related to Israel or the church, forty instances are general references to the church, and only in two instances is there any direct reference to ethnic Israel, and those are recounting historical events that occurred long before Jesus prophesied the *ekklesia* He would build upon Himself. The NT use of the term *ekklesia* provides no support for Israel and the church as interchangeable, but instead provides sixty-eight specific instances of support for the distinctiveness of the church from ethnic or geographical Israel. Further, the term does not accommodate any assertion that the church is spiritual Israel.

Collectively these four evidences answer the question of whether or not the Biblical data, understood through the literal grammatical historical hermeneutic, support the complete and ongoing distinction of Israel and the church. When applied to the Biblical data, each of the four methodological and hermeneutical issues considered here – authorial intention, progressive revelation, historical context, and lexical context – are resounding in their support for the complete and ongoing distinction of Israel and the church.

15
PRIORITY OF HERMENEUTICS IN APPLICATION AND ETHICS:
THE DISJUNCT BETWEEN DESCRIPTIVE AND PRESCRIPTIVE[289]

The short-form process of discerning and appropriating the meaning of a Biblical passage includes the four basic steps of (1) observation, (2) interpretation, (3) correlation, and (4) application. The more detailed process exegetical process includes nine steps: (1) verify text and translation, (2) understand background and context, (3) identify structural keys, (4) identify grammatical and syntactical keys, (5) identify lexical keys, (6) identify Biblical context, (7) identify theological context, (8) secondary verification, and (9) exposition.

Steps one through seven of the detailed exegetical process correspond to observation and interpretation in the more summary process. Both methods include a verification element, and both culminate with appropriation (exposition and application). Compared side by side, the processes coincide as follows:

---

[289] Adapted from "The Hermeneutical and Exegetical Implications of Descriptive and Prescriptive" in *Integrating Exegesis and Exposition* (Fort Worth, TX: Exegetica Publishing, 2015).

Abbreviated Process	*Detailed Process*
Observation	Verify text and translation
	Understand background and context
	Identify structural keys
	Identify grammatical and syntactical keys
	Identify lexical keys
	Identify Biblical context
	Identify theological context
Interpretation	(Result of the seven observational steps)
Correlation	Secondary verification
Application	Exposition

As a result of the seven observational or exegetical steps, we can formulate and test our interpretation, and we can appropriate the passage properly. The exposition of a passage includes a discussion of the applications of a passage, and should include some consideration of primary and secondary application. Primary application refers to how the original audience was to respond to the passage, while secondary application references expected responses of later (i.e., secondary) readers.

The distinction between the two aspects (primary and secondary) is critical. Without acknowledging the distinction, we would not be able to discern whether or not we (the modern readers), for example, are expected to go to a nearby village to obtain the colt of a donkey (Mt 21:2). All seven observational steps help us differentiate between primary and secondary application, as we discover what is descriptive and what is prescriptive. Descriptive is that which describes, as in historical narrative. Acts 5:1-11, for example, describes what took place when Ananias and Sapphira lied in order to make themselves look more spiritual. Prescriptive is that which prescribes, or commands. Prescriptive material is that which provides directions for the audience. Matthew 28:18-20 contains one prescription, the imperative to make disciples (*matheteusate*). Further, because this imperative is in a descriptive context (the passage is describing what Jesus said to His disciples), we can recognize that the passage is describing a prescription for the disciples, and thus the primary application of the passage was a call for the disciples to obey the specific command. We can certainly draw a secondary application from this passage, from the description of the events that took place there, and from other Biblical contexts which focus on disciplemaking (eg., 2 Tim 2:2). But the primary application of this passage is for the disciples to whom Jesus was speaking – just as in Matthew 21:2, the primary application is for the specific disciples Jesus was addressing (thus we are not obligated to obtain the colt of a donkey).

In considering primary and secondary applications, the first question to be asked is whether or not the passage is descriptive or prescriptive. Next, if the passage is prescriptive, we need to ask for whom is it prescriptive? Consider Exodus 19:4-6, as an example:

> 'You yourselves have seen what I did to the Egyptians, and *how* I bore you on eagles' wings, and brought you to Myself. 'Now then, if you will indeed obey My voice and keep My covenant, then you shall be My own possession among all

the peoples, for all the earth is Mine; and you shall be to Me a kingdom of priests and a holy nation.' These are the words that you shall speak to the sons of Israel.

These verses are descriptive, in that they are the record of what God said to Moses (see 19:3). They are also prescriptive in the sense that they contain information Moses was commanded to pass along to Israel. So in answer to the question regarding the recipient of the prescription, the answer is Moses. There appears to be another prescriptive layer here, as the content was to be heeded by Israel ("...hear My voice and keep My covenant..."), but it is not until the message is delivered that it becomes prescriptive for Israel. So we might identify the primary application as for Moses to communicate what God spoke. There are a number of secondary applications we might draw from this description of Moses' prescription, but only one primary application. Further in 19:7 we read a description of Moses fulfilling the prescription of 19:3, and delivering God's message to Israel. The primary application of 19:7 would be for Israel to respond to what was given them. Again, we might draw any number of secondary applications, but the primary application is limited to the initial audience.

In considering the distinction between descriptive and prescriptive, it is evident that we need to identify the direct recipient of any prescriptions so that we can properly apply (primary) the passage. Once we have done that we can move on to the more descriptive elements that would lead us to secondary applications. Let's examine one more example. Consider Acts 16:11-34, the account of the Philippian jailor coming to believe in Christ. The context is descriptive, as it is a narrative describing events that happened. This is most obvious from the use of past tense and the sequence of the events as they are described. However, in 16:31 we discover a prescriptive element in response to the jailor's question of what he must do to be saved. Paul and Silas responded that he should believe (*pisteuson*, aorist active imperative, second person singular) in the Lord Jesus. In order to correctly apply the passage, we must identify who is the recipient of the prescription. In this case, it is the Philippian Jailor.

The primary application of the prescription is then that the jailor needed to believe in order to be saved. It is not correct to apply the passage as a universal formula for salvation – even *if the conditions are universally applicable*. The primary application of the prescription is not to you and me; rather it was for the Philippian jailor. Now, of course we might draw many appropriate secondary applications, as we recognize that the formula is indeed universally applicable (all who believe in Jesus Christ has eternal life, see, Jn 6:47, for example), but we need to be careful to distinguish between the primary application and the secondary. In instances like these we must keep in mind that arriving at a proper conclusion (in this case, what one must do to be saved) does not justify misapplying a passage.

As part of the interpretation process, we must recognize descriptive and prescriptive language, distinguishing between the two. In so doing we will have a much clearer understanding of primary and secondary applications in a given context.

16
PRIORITY OF HERMENEUTICS IN SOCIO-POLITICAL THOUGHT:
THE NECESSITY OF PREMILLENNIALISM[290]

Dispensationalists have been accused of, among other things,[291] being pessimistic (as by Marsden and Bube)[292] and

---

[290] Originally presented to the Council on Dispensational Hermeneutics as "Biblical Derived Premillennialism as a Necessary Condition for a Biblical Socio-Political Model," Kansas City, Missouri, September, 2014.
[291] Tweeted by @Ligioner, 1/20/2012, 8:26pm: "Why aren't you a dispensationalist?" R.C. Sproul replied, "Because I think that dispensational theology is goofy." http://www.ligonier.org/blog/twitter-highlights-12212/; "Dispensational pre-millennialism typically causes a predisposition toward pessimism in world affairs and a general worsening of international relations. A pre-millennial reading of Bible prophecy paints a dismal picture of a world disintegrating toward a cataclysmic end where we are forced to confront the wrath and judgment of God. Assumptions and plans based on this worldview will be less than ideal" (Major Brian L. Stuckert, "Strategic Implications of American Millennialism," Monograph submitted to School of Advanced Military Studies United States Army Command and General Staff College Fort Leavenworth, Kansas, 2008.).
[292] "This view [premillennialism] emphasizes the pessimism of the present day, in which we can look forward to nothing more than continued degradation of the world and disintegration of human society until Christ returns to establish justice and righteousness by His power" (Richard H. Bube, "Optimism and Pessimism: Science and Eschatology, in *JETS*, Fall 1972; 217.); "The area where dispensationalists were perhaps most out of step with the rest of nineteenth-century thinking was in their view of contemporary history, which had little or no room for social or political progress. When they spoke on this question,

anti-semitic (as by Wilson),[293] in large part due to the premillennial understanding of Biblical eschatology. However, upon exegetical consideration of several foundational prerequisites of Biblical socio-political thought, it is evident that Biblical socio-political undergirding in fact *requires* the premillennial understanding, and that such an understanding affords dispensationalists an appropriate (i.e., Biblical) degree of care, realism, and constructiveness for the world around us. In short, owing much to the premillennial understanding, dispensational thinking – far from being a hindrance to the progress of society, is a great benefit to society. This has profound and far-reaching practical implications not only for dispensational thought, but also for practical ministry in the church and for interaction with those outside the church.

Prolegomena

A Biblical worldview, by definition, must include at least two characteristics: (1) it must be Biblical – derived exclusively from the Biblical record, and (2) it must be, in fact, a worldview – that is to say it should be, as Vidal puts it, a "collection of concepts allowing us to 'construct a global image of the world, and in this way to understand as many elements of our

---

dispensational premillennialists were characteristically pessimistic" (George Marsden, *Fundamentalism and American Culture: The Shaping of Twentieth Century Evangelicalism 1870-1925* (Oxford: Oxford University Press, 1980), 66.).

[293] "It is regrettable that this view [that Gentiles are occasionally instruments of God's retribution on Israel] allowed premillennialists to expect the phenomenon of anti-Semitism and tolerate it matter-of-factly" (Dwight Wilson, *Armageddon Now! The Premillenarian Response to Russia and Israel Since 1917* (Tyler, TX: Institute for Christian Economics, 1991), 16.).

experience as possible.'"[294] Vidal's characterization of worldview is consistent with the German concept of *Weltanshauung*[295] as foundational, internally cohesive, and comprehensive – three important traits for a *meaningful* worldview.

Foundational

A Biblical worldview should be foundational, in that it works from the ground up. This is a challenge for historical dispensationalism, which has been largely considered an extraction from Reformed theology with but a few reformations of its own. Rather than viewing dispensational thought as a Biblical outworking that stands independently and as constructed purely on Biblical foundations, we sometimes perceive dispensationalism as a refocusing of Reformed theology especially in the areas of eschatology and ecclesiology.[296] But as we begin to acknowledge that dispensationalism is not a hermeneutic through which we view the Bible, but is instead the result of the Bible examined through a particular method (the literal grammatical historical hermeneutic), we may recognize the necessity of attending to the foundational aspects of dispensational thought instead of simply borrowing foundations from other theological traditions.

---

[294] C. Vidal, (2008) Wat is een wereldbeeld? (What is a worldview?), in Van Belle, H. & Van der Veken, J., Editors, *Nieuwheid denken. De wetenschappen en het creatieve aspect van de werkelijkheid,* in press. Acco, Leuven; 3.

[295] German: worldview.

[296] Perhaps this is one reason dispensationalism has lacked historically in the development of worldview in favor of works on ecclesiology and eschatology.

Internally Cohesive

A Biblical worldview must also be internally cohesive, in that its components should fit together and should progress in some logical sequence. Much like Paul describes the church as built on the cornerstone that is Christ and on the foundation of the apostles and prophets, and as being built up with all the saints, there is a logical flow and interconnectedness in a meaningful worldview. That progress demands an internal consistency in the sense that one area of examination cannot contradict another without the whole being undermined. If one logically necessary subset fails, then the category that birthed the subset is flawed and untenable with respect to truth. Because a Biblical worldview purports to be grounded in *truth*, any single inconsistency within the system breaks down the whole system as untrustworthy. Hence, consistency is paramount in the development of this or any other system.

Comprehensive

In light of the global implications of *Weltanshauung*, a Biblical worldview must be comprehensive in that if it is derived from a source that claims to be sufficient for the adequacy and equipping of its believers for every good work (2 Tim 3:16-17), it must, in fact, be sufficient to that end, lest it violate (1) the principle of internal cohesiveness or consistency and (2) its own foundational truth claim. Consequently, the jurisdiction of a Biblical worldview is unlimited, and there is no field of inquiry on which the Bible cannot shed at least some foundational light. It is in this sense that Ryrie suggests that the Scriptures provide a comprehensive philosophy of history. His comments to this effect are worth consideration here:

> The Scriptures per se are not a philosophy of history, but they contain one. It is true that the Bible deals with ideas- but with ideas that are interpretations of historical events. This interpretation of the meaning of historical events is the task of theology, and it is a task that is not without its problems. The chief problem is that both covenant and dispensational theologies claim to represent the true philosophy of history as contained in the Scriptures. The problem is further complicated by the fact that, if a philosophy of history is defined as "a systematic interpretation of universal history in accordance with a principle by which historical events and successions are unified and directed toward ultimate meaning," then in a certain sense both systems of theology meet the basic requirements of the definition. However, the way in which the two systems meet these requirements affirms that dispensationalism is the more valid and helpful system. Notice that the definition centers on three things: (1) the recognition of "historical events and successions," or a proper concept of the progress of revelation in history; (2) the unifying principle; and (3) the ultimate goal of history. Let us examine both systems in relation to these three features.[297]

Notice Ryrie's (correct) perception that theology needs to be more broadly explanatory than simply offering commentary on a few religious issues, that it is closely related to philosophy, and that of the two major models (dispensationalism and covenant

---

[297] Charles C. Ryrie, *Dispensationalism*, Revised and Expanded (Chicago, IL: Moody Press, 1995), 16.

theology) which attempt to account for human experience, dispensationalism offers the best philosophy of history. Ryrie's thoughts here underscore the importance of a foundational, internally cohesive, and fully comprehensive model, and he asserts that dispensationalism is the best model in those regards.

Components and Grounding of a Biblical Worldview

Recognizing seven particular components is helpful for addressing the necessity for a worldview to be both foundational and comprehensive. In logical order of consideration from the perspective of the inquirer,[298] we undertake these seven steps as they build successively on each other – each being grounded on the conclusions of the previous step. (1) Epistemology, as the study of knowledge and the first step in the worldview inquiry, helps us arrive at understanding how we can know with certainty the answers all the other steps. In short, epistemology considers the source of authority for all other inquiry. (2) Ontology builds on that foundation by appealing to the source of authority confirmed in the epistemological inquiry, and explains what is the reality around us. Ontology is the inquiry about what actually exists. (3) Teleology explains why that which exists does indeed exist. Teleology considers purpose, and relies wholly on the epistemological conclusions for its basis. (4) Eschatology is only possible insofar as the epistemological source of authority

---

[298] Or course, the perspective of the inquirer isn't always the best perspective. In this discussion we consider epistemology before metaphysical issues, because the epistemological question must be addressed first by the inquirer in order to understand the metaphysical question. However, the metaphysical reality exists with or without the inquirer's understanding, and thus comes first in reality. This issue is addressed in *Appendix I*.

reveals what the future will hold, and is a necessary prerequisite to worldview components pertaining to human practice, because the concepts of reward and consequence are purely eschatological. (5) Axiology answers questions regarding value and the nature of good and evil, and is closely akin to teleology, as purpose determines function and makes obvious what is good and what is not. (6) Praxeology moves the inquirer from *is* to *ought* – from descriptive to prescriptive – and serves as the *therefore* in the worldview series of inquiry. The term praxeology, as employed here, refers to the behavior and ethics required of individuals by the axiological conclusions. (7) Sociopraxy extrapolates praxeological conclusions to the societal level: whereas praxeology considers ethics on an individual level, sociopraxy considers ethical obligations on a societal level.

These seven components fit within four major categories of philosophical pursuit: epistemology, metaphysics (includes ontology, teleology, eschatology, and axiology), ethics (praxeology), and socio-political thought (sociopraxy). It is worth noting how much of our inquiry is in the realm of metaphysics, and that in order to answer questions pertaining to metaphysics, we must have tools that are capable of addressing the metaphysics questions. Thus, epistemology is the foundational first field of inquiry.

Epistemology

Before we can take the first step in constructing (or understanding) a meaningful worldview we must discern the basis for recognizing what is true and what is not true. Without such a basis, any further pursuit is devoid of meaning, and we are left with no means to answer questions. All meaningful answers, then, are necessarily rooted in the concept of authority, and the questions themselves invite us to consider what are the overarching principles that govern our human experience.

Historically there have been many attempts at deciphering those overarching principles, but a few stand out as particularly influential. Plato's dualism (as represented by his allegory of the cave and his divided-line theory from *The Republic,* Book VII) suggests that the realm of experience offers only cursory glances at truth, but that greater enlightenment through the gaining of knowledge is necessary for the discerning of more certain truth. Plato's epistemology prescribed philosophical learning and reasoning as the path to certainty. Rene Descartes' rationalism (as represented in his *Discourse on the Method of Rightly Conducting the Reason and Seeking Truth in the Sciences*) prescribes the guided (by Descartes' method) use of human reason as the means of determining truth. David Hume's empiricism (as discussed in his *Treatise on Human Nature*) relies on human experience interpreted by the senses for the discernment of truth. Hume makes no allowance for the supernatural or metaphysical, because he asserts we possess no tools to sense these things. Thus for Hume reality is grounded in the natural, in what we can sense. Nietzsche abandoned the cause of the discernment of truth as grounding for meaningful worldview. Instead he pursued his existentialist course that the only thing of which we can be certain is that any true meaning is inaccessible to us and thus irrelevant.[299] Consequently, we make our own meaning by being the best version of us we can be.

The epistemological conclusions of each of these thinkers share one thing in common: *unapologetic self-reliance for the*

---

[299] E.g., as in *Thus Spoke Zarathustra.*

determining of truth. Plato relies on his understanding, Descartes on his reason, Hume on his senses, and Nietzsche on his will to power. In stark contrast, the Bible prescribes a model antithetical to the self-reliance prescribed in the aforementioned epistemological models.

The first epistemological statement in the Bible is actually made by the serpent in the Garden: "For God knows that in the day you eat from it your eyes will be opened, and you will be like God, knowing good and evil" (Gen 3:5). Satan prescribes knowledge through contradicting God's design for knowledge. The fact that Satan chose epistemology as an early battleground underscores the strategic significance of epistemology in God's design. In this context Satan challenges Eve to consider a different starting point than God had prescribed, and if she does, Satan promises, Eve will have a better outcome – that her knowledge will be more complete, even to the point of making her godlike. While the actions Satan prescribed did result in particular knowledge (Gen 3:22), it was a distortion of God's design for knowledge and resulted in tragedy and not blessing.

These events invite the reader to inquire as to God's ideal for human knowledge, and the answer is provided especially in the writings of Solomon, to whom it was granted to be exceedingly wise (1 Kin 3:12). In the book of Proverbs Solomon identifies the first epistemological step undergirding a Biblical worldview: "The fear of the Lord is the beginning of wisdom" (Prov 1:7); "The fear of the Lord is the beginning of wisdom, and the knowledge of the Holy One is understanding" (Prov 9:10); and again, "The fear of the Lord is the instruction for wisdom" (Prov 15:33). The word for *fear* is the Hebrew *yirah*, and does not simply denote respect, but is the term normally used of *fear* – as in fear for one's life.[300] In context, the fear of the Lord involves the right perspective of and response to God.[301] Though Solomon uses a different word for *fear* in Proverbs 28:14, the contrast to appropriate fear is hardness of heart.[302] In short, the fear of the Lord involves the inner man's responsiveness to God.

Notice the critique of the atheist in Psalm 14:1: "The fool has said in his heart (Heb., *leb*) 'There is no God.'" The fool is unresponsive toward God, and sets his will against God, whereas the one who would possess wisdom acknowledges God and is responsive to Him. From whence comes the fear of the Lord? "For the Lord gives wisdom; from His mouth comes wisdom and understanding" (Prov 2:6). If the first step or first principle of Biblical epistemology is to fear the Lord, the authoritative source for the data we need to do so is identified as Scripture itself – a revelation which presupposes the existence of the Biblical God, and makes no effort to defend that first and most vital principle.

As we read the Bible, we discover therein the limitations of human reasoning, and thus, the inadequacies of learning and rationalism (Gen 6:5; 1 Cor 2:14); we encounter the limited scope of human experience and of the uninformed arrogance of naturalistic empiricism (Job 38:4, 34-35, 39:26-27, 41:11, 42:5-6); and we are met with the reality that there is indeed discernable meaning and truth – noumenal reality, created and revealed by God, and relevant for everyday human life – even if

---

[300] E.g., Gen 15:1, 32:11; Prov 3:25, etc.
[301] Discussions regarding the fear the Lord are found also in the NT in passages such as Romans 3:18; 2 Corinthians 5:11, 7:1; Ephesians 5:21; 1 Peter 2:17; and Revelation 14:7.
[302] The Hebrew *leb*, translated here as *heart*, is generally used to reference the heart, mind, will, and/or inner man.

God hasn't revealed its fullness (Ecc 3:11; Jn 20:31; Jam 3:17-18; 1 Jn 5:13).[303] *A Biblical worldview starts with a Biblical epistemology, which identifies the Bible itself as the source of authority for all other inquiries, in contradistinction to any other proposed source of authority.*[304]

The Hermeneutic Requirement of a Biblical Epistemology

Interpretive method is an integral factor in applying a Biblical epistemology. If the fear of the Lord is the beginning of wisdom (Prov 1:7), and if wisdom is knowable and discernible (Prov 1:2), then the fear of the Lord is knowable and discernible. If knowledge and understanding come from His mouth (Prov 2:6), and if knowledge and understanding are rooted in the fear of the Lord (Prov 9:10), then the fear of the Lord is discovered in

---

[303] Much of the material from the previous four paragraphs is adapted from Christopher Cone, "Epistemological Foundations of a Biblical Theology, or Bob's Crazy Day with the Dandelions" presented to the Chafer Theological Seminary Conference, March 12, 2014, and later published online at http://www.drcone.com/2014/03/13/epistemological-foundations-for-a-Biblical-theology/.

[304] One critique of this epistemological first-principle (that the Bible is the authoritative source of truth) is that it amounts to fideism or circular reasoning. But that charge rings hollow when one recognizes that all epistemological first-principle claims (whether by Plato, Descartes, Hume, Nietzsche, or anyone else) are assumed to be self-authenticating and self-evident by those who make the claims. The very first step in any worldview system is necessarily understood to be self-evident (or else it would obviously be a second step, not a first), and its legitimacy as first-principle is generally tested by how well it corresponds to truth (correspondence theory), by the resulting worldview's internal cohesiveness and coherence (coherence theory), and for some, by how well the system actually works (pragmatic theory). I suggest that the Biblical worldview holds up well under the scrutiny of any of the three traditional theories of truth, and that the Biblical epistemological first-principle is no more circular in its reasoning than is the first-principle of any competing epistemological system.

His word. If these two syllogisms are valid and true, then the word of God (at least insofar as it considers the fear of the Lord) is knowable and discernible.

Even a cursory examination of Scripture gives us at least two major evidences that the Bible intends its readers to employ a particular hermeneutic method in discerning the meaning of the Bible. First, the Bible is written using three distinct human languages (Hebrew, Aramaic, and Greek), each with its own distinctive grammatical structures and vocabulary. The simple fact that these languages are employed demands that the reader respect fundamental aspects of the languages and follow literal grammatical historical principles. In order to have knowable and discernible meaning, any written communication employing human language requires this.

Second, the first two-thousand years of recorded history demonstrate that the literal grammatical historical hermeneutic was exclusively used. In the first twelve chapters of the Genesis narrative (a section of Scripture which covers roughly two thousand years), we find some thirty-one occurrences of the phrases "God said," "the Lord God said," and "the Lord said." In all but possibly one instance the listener responds to God's word as if understanding God in the natural, normative way the employed language describes. The light comes into existence, just as God commanded (1:3). Everything else during creation week employs the same hermeneutic. Even God Himself uses the literal grammatical historical hermeneutic: He describes how He will make man (1:26), and then He does exactly what He said (1:27). After the Fall, Adam and Eve still understand that God means exactly what He says, as they respond directly to His questions, understanding them through the same hermeneutic lens as before (3:9, 14). God gives Noah specific instruction, commanding him to build a precisely designed boat (6:14-21). Thankfully, Noah did not employ an allegorical or spiritualized hermeneutic as he took God's words for what they were and did exactly what God had told him to do (6:22). Finally, God told Abram to go (12:1), and Abram did exactly as God told him (12:4).

The only potential recorded exception to the two-thousand year rule is found in 3:1, where the serpent challenges what was God said. Even in this, the serpent doesn't specifically employ a different hermeneutic method, but he does challenge the truth of what was said (3:4) and God's motivation in saying it (3:5). In short the only one who is recorded to have questioned or challenged God's meaning during the first two-thousand years of history is the serpent. These chapters provide a clear indicator of how God intends to be understood, and underscore the difficulty encountered when the simple meaning of the communication is not followed. Based on at least these two evidences (linguistic and historical) the literal grammatical historical hermeneutic is *sine qua non* to a Biblical epistemology. Without simplicity and univocality in meaning, there can be no Biblical epistemology (at least not as Solomon describes it). Simply put, along with the other components of epistemology, the Bible prescribes a knowable and discernible hermeneutic method for its readers.[305]

---

[305] While there may be some later instances in which the NT writer retasked an OT passage, those instances do not alter the initial meaning. In Matthew 2:15, for example, the event described in Hosea 11:1 is newly revealed as a foreshadowing of Christ, but the clear statement of Hosea 11:1 still stands, and Israel is still the referent. It is important to realize that in such instances the NT writers are generally *using* the text, not reinterpreting it. However, even if in some instances there *actually were* redefinition, it would seem the prerogative of a Divine author to handle

Eschatological Implications of a Biblical Epistemology

Employing a Biblical epistemology, we can discern from Scripture a Biblical metaphysic. With respect to ontology, God the Father (Eph 4:6), God the Son (Jn 1:1, 1 Cor 8:6), and God the Holy Spirit (Gen 1:2, Jn 14:26) exist. Creation exists (Gen 1:1). Mankind exists (Gen 1:27). Angels exist (Gen 19:1). Satan exists (Rev 12:9). With respect to a Biblical teleology, all things are purposed simply for His glory (e.g., Num 14:21). With respect to axiology, ultimate value is not an intrinsic thing but rather an instrumental one, since it requires an Ultimate Valuer. Therefore God's ultimate purpose has to be considered when trying to understand what is good. That which God declares is good, *is good*, and it seems He determines what is good based on how it contributes to His overall doxological purpose (e.g., Heb 13:21).

The questions of ontology, teleology, and axiology provide relatively simple answers, because, in the case of ontology things either exist or they don't; in the case of teleology, there is much Biblical data on the ultimate purpose of all things; and in the case of axiology, value is simply determined by the teleolology: that which God declares is good, is good for accomplishing the purpose of His glory, and is therefore good to Him – the Ultimate Valuer.

Eschatology is a bit unique in comparison to ontology and teleology, however, as the eschatological data is so voluminous, and considers so many prophetic events. The questions of eschatology are far more complex than those of ontology and

---

things as He so desires, but He never extends that prerogative to the interpreter, instead there is a clear and normative precedent for grammatical historical understanding throughout the Biblical revelation.

teleology. Still, historically, eschatology has been distilled into three basic interpretive traditions: premillennialism, postmillennialism, and amillennialism. Advocates of postmillennialism and amillennialism continue to readily admit that their views are supported by the occasional use of non-literal hermeneutics.[306] Some, such as Kevin DeYoung, advocate for reading one's theological system into the text in order to support the views of that system. DeYoung questions rhetorically, "Without a systematic theology how can you begin to know what to do with the eschatology of Ezekiel or the sacramental language in John 6 or the psalmist's insistence that he is righteous and blameless?"[307] Likewise, critics of premillennialism admit, along with Louis Berkhof, that dispensational premillennialism is only defensible if a literal grammatical historical hermeneutic is employed.[308]

Still, it is evident that premillennialism is not *the foundational issue* in a Biblical worldview, and is not even *the pivotal issue* in eschatology. Rather premillennialism is a metaphysics-category outworking of epistemology, ontology, teleology, and axiology. John Piper's optimistic premillennialism (similar to covenant premillennialism),[309] for example, can still

---

[306] E.g., Sam Storms, "Why I Changed My Mind on the Millennium" at http://thegospelcoalition.org/article/why-i-changed-my-mind-about-the-millennium.

[307] Kevin DeYoung, "Your Theological System Should Tell You How to Exegete" at http://thegospelcoalition.org/blogs/kevindeyoung/2012/02/23/your-theological-system-should-tell-you-how-to-exegete/.

[308] Louis Berkhof, *Systematic Theology*, 4th Revised and Enlarged Edition (Grand Rapids, MI: Eerdmans, 1941), 706-715.

[309] Matt Perman, "What does John Piper believe about dispensationalism, covenant theology, and new covenant theology?" at

be classified as premillennialism, yet his sociopraxy includes a non-cessationist approach consistent with Daniel Fuller's revelational/non-revelational view on inerrancy,[310] and Wayne Grudem's more recent "middle ground"[311] non-cessationist approach that suggests that the gift of prophecy does not always result in inerrant declarations, and that even Biblical prophecy can sometimes be "a bit wrong."[312] Piper admits to being "significantly influenced" by Grudem's view.[313] This aspect of (ecclesiological) sociopraxy is incompatible with the foundational epistemological principles of a Biblical worldview, in that this particular brand of non-cessationism alleges essentially that there are incorrect statements in Biblical prophecy. Notably, Piper advocates testing New Testament prophecy to determine if it is "good."[314]

The point here is that one can draw a basic premillennial conclusion without building it on the Biblical epistemological basis, and that resulting aspects of sociopraxy (as in Fuller's, Grudem's, and Piper's case) will not necessarily be compatible with Biblical epistemological grounding. Consequently, premillennialism (or the lack thereof) is simply not the issue. *How premillennialism is arrived at is of central importance here.* Thus it is fair to say that a Biblically derived

---

http://www.desiringgod.org/articles/what-does-john-piper-believe-about-dispensationalism-covenant-theology-and-new-covenant-theology.
[310] Daniel Fuller, "Benjamin B. Warfield's View of Faith and History" in Evangelical Theological Society *Bulletin*, Vol. II, No. 2, Spring 1968: 80.
[311] Wayne Grudem, *The Gift of Prophecy in the New Testament and Today* (Wheaton, IL: Crossway, 2000), 17.
[312] Ibid., 79.
[313] John Piper "What is the Gift of Prophecy in the New Covenant" podcast, at http://www.desiringgod.org/blog/posts/piper-on-prophecy-and-tongues, 1:00.
[314] Ibid., 1:48.

premillennialism is a necessary outworking of a Biblical epistemology and a necessary condition for a Biblical sociopraxy. In other words, Biblically derived premillennialism is simply one domino in a long sequence of dominoes in a Biblical worldview. If premillennialism is Biblically derived,[315] it will carry with it key components unique to dispensational premillennialism that are foreign to covenant and other forms of dispensational premillennialism, including the complete distinction between Israel and the church and the absence of the church in the Old Testament. In short, Biblically derived premillennialism will cause other distinctive dominoes to fall.

Socio-Political Implications
Of Biblically Derived Premillennialism

Having established a Biblical epistemology and the necessary connection between a Biblical epistemology and a Biblical metaphysic (including the elements of ontology, teleology, eschatology, and axiology), we have focused a bit more directly on premillennialism, as opposed to other eschatological principles. Moving from the is^{316} category (including epistemology and metaphysics) to the $ought^{317}$ category (including praxeology or ethics, and sociopraxy or socio-political thought) we examine some of the implications of a Biblically derived premillennialism, as it pertains specifically to sociopraxy.

As mentioned at the outset, characterizations of dispensational premillennialism as a negative socio-political

---

[315] See Appendix II, for a summary of how premillennialism is supported by the Hebrew Prophets.
[316] Or, descriptive.
[317] Or, prescriptive.

influence have included charges of pessimism and anti-semitism. There are of course many other indictments against dispensational premillenialism, but these two are answered here simply to demonstrate the internal cohesiveness of the Biblical worldview as it pertains to Biblically derived premillenialism.

Pessimism

It is certainly true that Biblical prophecy, literally understood, does not paint an optimistic picture for the future of the world: "...the earth and its works will be burned up" (2 Pet 3:10b). Revelation adds that future events will include a third of all trees and grass being destroyed (8:7), a third of all life in the sea dying (8:9), a third of all freshwaters becoming toxic (8:11), a third of the sun, moon, and stars being darkened (8:12). If the interpreter is working from a Biblical epistemology, which requires a literal grammatical historical hermeneutic, the interpreter must acknowledge that these things are coming at some point in the future.

But there is a tremendous distinction between an eschatologically pessimistic metaphysic regarding the present form of the heavens and earth and a pessimistic sociopraxy. The question at issue is whether or not a so-called pessimistic metaphysic must necessarily result in a pessimistic praxeology and/or sociopraxy. The Bible answers this question in the negative. In fact, the coming negative events are cited by Biblical writers for the express purpose of calling believers to optimistic action.

Peter, after describing coming cataclysms and the restoration to follow, exhorts believers to look for these things and in the meantime to "be diligent to be found by Him in peace, spotless and blameless, and regard the patience of our Lord to be salvation..." (2 Pet 3:14-15a). Earlier in the context Peter explains that the Lord's patience has to do with His "not wishing for any to perish but for all to come to repentance" (2 Pet 3:9). Likewise, the book of Revelation is addressed to the churches (Rev 22:16), and includes multiple ethical and sociopractical exhortations (e.g., 2:5, 2:10, 2:16, 2:25, 3:3, 3:18-20). While Revelation does not provide any specific socio-political imperatives, Peter's writings do.

Despite what some might call metaphysic pessimism, Peter mandates that believers keep their behavior excellent so that those who observe will glorify God (1 Pet 2:12). Peter calls on believers to be submissive to government and to treat all men with honor (1 Pet 2:12-17). Finally, Peter asserts that the prophesied future is a basis for godliness and goodness (e.g., 1 Pet 4). Paul considers similar themes in Romans 12-13 and 2 Timothy 3. Rather than being pessimistic in his own actions and those he prescribes of others, Paul has a vigorous sense of urgency to serve well, to be faithful, and to be a benefit to all around him for the sake of their eternal good (e.g., 1 Cor 9:14-23).

In short, the Biblical pessimism about the imminent future is a basis for believers' selfless and beneficent conduct of life, as believers anticipate the ultimate eternal future. Consequently, the criticism of Biblically derived premillennialism as promoting pessimistic praxeology and sociopraxy falls in the straw-man category of fallacies, as such allegations confuse the *is* with the *ought*. To illustrate, the ontological reality that it is highly likely that your ice cream will melt soon is not grounds for your pessimism. In fact, it is quite the opposite. It provides you with an urgency based in truth, and grounding for doing the right thing with the ice cream while you have the opportunity.

Anti-Semitism

Wilson's critique of dispensational premillennialism is likewise a conflating of *is* and *ought*, as he assumes that the prophetic expectation of anti-Semitism naturally leads to the sociopractical tolerance of anti-Semitism. On the assertion that dispensationalism expects a future anti-Semitism, Wilson is correct. Revelation 12:13, in context, describes a Satanic effort to destroy the Jews. Clearly if Satan is leading that charge it would be odd that anyone would think the church would be complicit in such efforts. Yet, history does not lie in connecting the historical organization of the "church" with anti-Semitism. From Chrysostom's *Eight Homilies against the Jews* to Luther's *The Jews and Their Lies* to the comments of numerous popes, there is no shortage of historical material demonstrating the "church's" displeasure with the Jewish people. But the grand irony here is that it is not dispensational premillennialism, but reformed and replacement theology that is historically guilty of anti-Semitic tendencies.

Yes, dispensational premillennialism interprets literally passages like Matthew 23:31-36 (Jesus speaking), Acts 2:36 (Peter speaking), and 1 Thessalonians 2:14-16 (Paul speaking) – passages which acknowledge that it was Jews who rejected Jesus and ultimately had Him crucified. But the point cannot be lost that during that same week when Jesus pronounced the Jews guilty, He died to pay for the sins of Israel and Judah under the terms of the New Covenant (Mt 26:28); it was Peter who encouraged those he indicted to change their minds about the Messiah, that they might be forgiven (Ac 2:28), and who later wrote to Jewish believers wishing them "grace and peace" in the fullest measure (1 Pet 1:3), and recounting Jesus' sacrifice in terms similar to Isaiah 53 (1 Pet 2:21-25), and so appealed to Jesus as the Jewish Messiah; and it was Paul who wrote to the Thessalonian believers – a church he founded by his preaching of the gospel to the Jewish people (Ac 17:1-4), and who proclaimed to the Romans that the good news of God's revealed righteousness was to the Jew first and then the Greek (Rom 1:16), and that consequences for evil (Rom 2:9), reward for doing good (Rom 2:10), and ultimately the good news of God's revealed righteousness (Rom 1:16) was to the Jew first and then to the Greek. And of course, all three men were Jewish. A literal reading of the text (as is required by a Biblical epistemology, and which undergirds Biblical eschatology and sociopraxy) allows absolutely no room for anti-semitism, nor advocates for any tolerance of it.

Conclusion

If hermeneutics is understood to be an integral component of epistemology, and if there is a knowable and discernible Biblical epistemology, then there is a knowable and discernible Biblical hermeneutic. If that hermeneutic is literal grammatical historical, and if premillennialism is an eschatological principle required by the literal grammatical historical model, then premillennialism is an eschatological principle required by a Biblical epistemology. Finally, if a Biblical model for sociopraxy is grounded in a Biblical epistemology, and if a Biblical worldview demands internal cohesiveness from its individual components, then the Biblical socio-political model must not contradict the epistemological principles upon which it stands.

Historically, Reformed epistemology departs from the syllogistic sequence above at the very first point. Cornelius Van Til illustrates the Reformed methodology of perceiving hermeneutics as separate from the epistemological discussion,[318] and this is the maneuver that allows for the occasional employment of non-literal hermeneutics. This is the maneuver that undergirds both the postmillennial and amillennial perspectives, and this is the maneuver that grounds the resulting socio-political systems.

In order to justify premillennialism, for example, we must attend to the epistemological grounding that supports it. In order to understand the implications of premillennialism, we must likewise consider the socio-political applications of the eschatological principle. In short, we must recognize that if dispensationalism is to have any explanatory value at all it must be representative of *the* Biblical worldview. Consequently, in our understanding of and development of dispensationalism, we cannot focus only on narrow categories out of sequence, but we must do the work required to discern a Biblical worldview which is Biblically derived, which is foundational in its sequence, which is internally cohesive, and which is comprehensive. Only then will the full weight of dispensationalism's explanatory value be felt.

APPENDIX I

The Premillennial Anticipation in the Hebrew Prophets

The Hebrew prophets anticipated (as they were told by God) that God would come to earth and rule over Israel as a

---

[318] See Appendix III.

representative in the Davidic line. Dispensational premillennialism has long understood Revelation 19-20 as a narrative of the fulfillment of those promises, and has been criticized by some for that understanding. The following discussion simply considers the anticipation of the Hebrew prophets regarding this future kingdom, as their prophecies form the contextual backdrop for the events of Revelation 19-20.

Isaiah 9:6-7

The Prince of Peace is both man (child, son, 9:6) and God (*el gabor*, Mighty God, 9:6). His government will be unlimited in increase and peace, and He will sit on the throne of David (9:7), to arrange or direct (*lehaqiyn*) it. This will be accomplished by the zeal of Yahweh Sabaoth. The establishment of the kingdom seems, in simplest terms, to be accomplished by this Messiah (or by Yahweh Sabaoth), and not by human agency (i.e., not by Israel or the church). Further, this kingdom is a literal kingdom in which this Messiah rules over the throne of David – David's kingdom was not a spiritual one, but a literal kingdom over Israel, centered primarily in Jerusalem.

Jeremiah 23:5-6

This prophecy speaks of a future time when a righteous branch will be raised for David (or on behalf of David), who will be a righteous king in the land of Israel (23:5). During His reign Judah and Israel will enjoy salvation and security, and He will be called Yahweh Tsidiqenu (The Lord our righteousness) (23:6). Considering the elements of this prophecy, the Lord will be a righteous king in the line of David, and in the land of David, consolidating the two kingdoms and bringing peace and security.

Jeremiah 30:7-9

Anticipating the great day of Jacob's trouble (30:7), this prophecy adds that Israel will no longer be under the yoke of others (30:8), but will serve God and David their king, who will be raised up for Israel (30:9). Here is yet another prophecy of national judgment and restoration, with the latter condition coming at a time when a Davidic king is ruling.

Jeremiah 33:15-26

A righteous branch of David (in this case, not David himself) is raised, and who executes justice and righteousness (33:15). Judah and Jerusalem will be saved during the administration of Yahweh Tsidiqenu (33:16). The enduring Davidic Kingdom (33:17) includes a Levitical priesthood (specifically the Zadokian line discussed in Ezek 40:46, 43:19, 44:15, and 48:11) (33:18). These things will take place as surely as the continuation of night and day (33:20-26).

Ezekiel 20:30-49

In a prophecy addressing the house of Israel directly (20:30), Adonai Yahweh declares that He will be king over Israel. He describes a physical regathering (20:34), a judgment (20:35-36), and an enacting of a covenant with Israel (20:37). This prophecy concludes with a call to action for that present generation of Israel, in light of the future rule of Yahweh Adonai from His holy mountain (e.g., 20:40). Ezekiel laments in the final verse that his listeners ignored the calls to action and considered the prophecy to be non-literal (20:49). It is evident from this prophecy that God intends to rule, literally, over Israel, in an economy governed by a covenant, and from His high mountain. In this context the regathering, the judgment, and the covenant all precede the ruling. Further it is notable that a non-literal understanding is explicitly frowned on.

Ezekiel 37:21-27

This prophecy begins with anticipation of a regathering (37:21) into the land of Israel, and the formerly separated kingdoms of North and South will be united under one king (37:22). David is referenced as king over them (37:24), and is also identified as their prince (37:25). David's status as king and prince (either in person or as representative of a royal line) does not invalidate earlier promises that God Himself would be king (e.g., 20:33). Associated with this rule is the establishing of a covenant of peace with Israel, a regathering, and a future with God present (37:26-27).

Daniel 2:34-35

The stone uncut by human hands first appears (2:34a), then strikes the feet mixed with iron and clay (2:34b), and then as the statue crumbles to dust, the stone grows to fill the whole earth (2:35). This sequential aspect is supported by the use of the vavs preceding the verbs for striking and filling. Simply put, the King appears, conquers the preceding kingdom, and then begins His rule. One could argue that the fifth kingdom begins with the striking of the fourth, but inarguably the stone actually appears before striking the statue and before filling the whole earth. This passage anticipates a pre-rule appearance of the fifth kingdom's King.

Daniel 9:24-27

The first verse in this pericope anticipates seven developments (to finish the transgression, to make an end of sin, to make atonement for iniquity, to bring in everlasting righteousness, to seal up vision and prophecy, and to anoint the holy of holies) during an allotted time sequence (i.e., seventy sevens). The sequence continues in verse 26 with Messiah being cut off after sixty-nine weeks, and desolations determined until the desolation of the Roman prince (who is to come) who makes and violates a seven-year covenant. There is no mention of a kingdom installed up to the point of that final desolation. If the destruction of the city refers to 70AD, then one who supports the view that the kingdom was somehow inaugurated with the advent of the church in 33AD must defend how times of desolations can be concurrent with the glorious rule of the Messiah. Gabriel's prediction here does not explicitly anticipate premillennialism, but it creates grand problems for the competing views of amillennialism and postmillennialism.

Zechariah 14:1-9

A day is coming in which what was taken from Israel will be returned (14:1). God Himself will gather the nations against Jerusalem, but ultimately God will *go forth* and fight against those nations (14:2-4). This will be a literal going forth, as He will stand on the Mount of Olives – changing its topography, and God will come with all the holy ones with Him (14:4-5). These events ultimately conclude with Yahweh as king over all the earth (14:9).

Conclusion

These are some passages that overtly anticipate God's kingdom coming to earth in physical, literal manifestation in the line of David, to rule not only over Israel, but also over the whole earth. In each case, the theme is the same: a regathering, judgment, and restoration of Israel under a Davidic king, who is ultimately God Himself. There is no textual reason at all to assume any of these references are to be understood in a non-literal way. In fact, the only time we see a non-literal response, that response is lamented (Ezek 20:49). From these passages it is evident that God would come to earth, in the Davidic line – appearing first, then meting out judgment and restoration, then ruling as king. These nine passages all support the premillennial coming of the Messiah, even if the details regarding the first segment of that kingdom as lasting one thousand years are not revealed until later (e.g., Rev 20:2-7).

Louis Berkhof famously criticized premillennialism, suggesting that "the Scriptural basis for this theory is Rev. 20:1-6, after an Old Testament meaning has been poured into it."[319] Despite Berkhof's criticism, it should be expected that in these final passages of Scripture the promises God made would be fulfilled. If Revelation 19-20 does not represent the fulfillment of these numerous and similar prophecies, then what would? Berkhof adds, "This passage occurs in a highly symbolic book and is admittedly very obscure...The literal interpretation of this passage...leads to a view that finds no support elsewhere in Scripture."[320] This author suggests that the literal interpretation of Revelation 19-20 is not at all obscure or symbolic, and is fully supported by each of the nine Hebrew prophecies discussed above.

---

[319] Louis Berkhof, *Systematic Theology*, 4th Revised and Enlarged Edition (Grand Rapids, MI: Eerdmans, 1941), 715.
[320] Ibid.

APPENDIX II

Cornelius Van Til is brilliant on what I would call the first three pillars of Biblical epistemology (#1: Biblical God exists, #2: He has revealed himself authoritatively, #3: Natural man's incapacity to receive), but his epistemology falls short in that he does not account for hermeneutics (Pillar #4) within his epistemology. In fact, in his Th.M thesis, "Reformed Epistemology," he never once even discusses Biblical interpretation. Much of his critique of other thinkers, like Kant, includes considerable discussion of their deficiencies in the interpretation of experience, but not a word about interpretation of Scripture. Not one.

How can Van Til build such an outstanding foundational framework on special revelation and then totally ignore the centrality of hermeneutic method for understanding that revelation? You see, it all has to do with where one places hermeneutics: Biblical hermeneutics is as an absolutely necessary component of epistemology. Hermeneutics falls within the realm of epistemology. Van Til does not seem to share that conviction, even though he critiques the hermeneutics of others' bases of authority (i.e., experience) within an epistemological context.

Still, while not considering hermeneutics an integral part of epistemology, he does give hermeneutics attention elsewhere. In his *The New Hermeneutic*, for example, Van Til concludes, with these words, "...we would appeal to the Cahier's men, to Wiersinga and to others, to build their hermeneutical procedures on the theology of Calvin, Kuyper, Bavinck, etc., (emphasis mine) and then in terms of it to challenge all men to repentance and faith in the self-identifying Christ of Scripture instead of making compromise with unbelief" (pp. 180). Notice his prescribed hermeneutical procedures are grounded in historical theology, rather than literal grammatical historical.

In short, Van Til is marvelously consistent in his epistemological method until he arrives at the hermeneutic component. At that point his writing shows, in my estimation, two deficiencies: (1) he does not grant hermeneutics its proper and necessary place in epistemology, and (2) when he does consider hermeneutics, he prescribes historical theology as the orthodox hermeneutic, rather than literal grammatical historical – an unfortunate contradiction of his own expertly stated first principles. The Biblical epistemological model does not share these two deficiencies, and leads me to consider that while Van Til is outstanding up to a point, we cannot simply adopt his reformed epistemology without ourselves walking more consistently down the reformed path. Premillennialism (and especially the dispensational form of premillennialism) demands its own epistemology, and one that includes hermeneutic method.

17
IMPLICATIONS OF PRIORITY IN HERMENEUTICS AND THEOLOGICAL METHOD

Five tools, three questions, two challenges, one ultimate source of truth...

Five Initial Tools at our Disposal

As we seek to discover, we observe that we possess basic tools useful for processing information: reason, the senses, emotion, desire/will, and instinct/innate awareness/conscience. We apply these five tools to the data, phenomena, or the things and events with which we interact. As we begin the process we aren't certain of which tools we can trust and to what extent, but in practical terms, we can only use what we have. So we march forward. We apply our tools to our own data, first accumulating enough information in context to form an opinion, and second, by borrowing the conclusions of others to expand our access to the data and to help speed up the process. We apply the tools in perhaps a tentative way at first, then as our worldview begins to take shape, we are willing to accept a higher level of commitment.

Three Questions to Answer

The tools fit in three categories, and thus demand that we address three major questions if we are to have a worldview that is coherent (internally consistent and non-contradictory, as in the coherency view of truth), corresponds to reality (as in the correspondence view of truth), and is workable (as in the pragmatic view of truth). The five tools of reason, senses, emotion, desire/will, and instinct/innate awareness/conscience can be categorized as pertaining to reason, experience, and meaning. Applying these five tools to the data implies three major needs: to satisfy reason, to explain experience, and to ascertain meaning.

Satisfying reason first demands the use of reason, but also applies the other four tools to interpret the data in a way that is coherent with reason. Explaining experience first demands the use of the senses, but also applies the other four tools to interpret the data in a way that corresponds to the reality of the phenomena. Ascertaining meaning employs instinct/innate awareness/conscience, desire/will, in cooperation with reason and the senses to recognize a workable reality – a reality that can be acted upon, and with purpose. Answering these three questions give us a perspective of reality and a direction to travel. They provide the *is* and *ought* of worldview.

Two Challenges to Following the Evidence

Pre-commitment versus following wherever the evidence leads can be a significant challenge in the worldview process. Longtime atheist Antony Flew spoke of pursuing wherever the evidence leads. When he moved from atheism to a form of theism, he recognized that his former atheist views had been more of a pre-commitment than an objective consideration of the evidence.[321] Few current atheists might admit such a high level of pre-commitment, though some have been willing to admit that their atheism is indeed a faith system. Some, like Carl Sagan, have made transparent pre-commitment statements like "the cosmos is all that is, ever was, and ever will be."[322] Statements like this step out of the scientific and move into the creedal, as there can be no verification of such assertions. Richard Lewontin maintains that there can be no "divine foot in the door,"[323] as he suggests there can't be any consideration of a supernatural answer. Lewontin's pre-commitment is not that different from some of the early Greek philosophers who sought to escape the pantheon and explain everything in exclusively naturalistic terms. Likewise, Biblical theist Ken Ham was steadfast that in the face of scientific evidence that conflicted with the Bible, he would defer to the Bible.[324] Arguably, there is pre-commitment on both sides of the issue, and while one's pre-commitment may ultimately turn out to be correct, in at least some senses it makes the process potentially more difficult.

Another challenge in the process is the potential to overemphasize one tool over others, to the detriment of objectivity. For example, if one follows an interpretation of the senses over and above that which satisfies reason, or *vice versa*, or if one follows an interpretation that emphasizes emotion over

---

[321] Antony Flew, *There Is A God: How The World's Most Notorious Atheist Changed His Mind* (Harper One, 2008).
[322] Carl Sagan, *The Cosmos* (Ballantine Books, 2013), 1.
[323] Richard Lewontin, "Billions and Billions of Demons," in The New York Review of Books, January 9, 1997, viewed at http://www.nybooks.com/articles/1997/01/09/billions-and-billions-of-demons/.
[324] Bill Nye vs. Kan Ham Debate, February 4, 2014, viewed at https://www.youtube.com/watch?v=z6kgvhG3AkI.

the senses, then there may be a tendency away from objectivity in favor of personal preference. Once again, this can take us back to pre-commitment. Christopher Hitchens said often that religion was humanity's first crack at interpreting reality. Arguably, it could be said that pre-modern thinking emphasized instinct or innate awareness over reason. Hitchens elevated the senses through science as a superior means of understanding, which represented (in my estimation) a pendulum swing too far, leading to an imbalance. In these cases, there are challenges for atheists and theists alike.

Applying the Tools to the Data, Addressing the Question

We find ourselves initially in possession of five tools with which to consider three questions. How can we satisfy reason, explain experience, and ascertain meaning? Ultimately what we are after is truth that corresponds to reality, that is coherent, and that is workable – truth that is *true*. We begin by observing what is around us, and we see systems. Systems of life, systems of order – organized, deliberate, and highly functional systems. With the five tools, we assess these systems tentatively.

With reason we think that these systems must exist, that they must have come from somewhere, and that there is a destination ahead. We suspect that they are discoverable, and that they are material for more thought and consideration. With the senses we can observe and interact, we can connect with systems and comprehend them on several levels, providing more data for our reason to consider. With emotion we see elegance and beauty in the systems – they are much more than cold realities. They are warm, alive, and reflective of something pleasing and endearing. There is not merely *impersonal*, there is *personal*. With desire and will we recognize that there is something meaningful about these systems that we want to engage and understand. We desire to be, and to use the tools we have in order to investigate and to discover. With instinct/innate awareness/conscience we sense that there is something (or Someone) behind the systems, that there is some purpose for them, and that we have some accountability for how we interact with them.

When we put these five together, we arrive at these tentative ideas: there is a personal reality with which we can interact, with which we are basically equipped to interact, with which we want to interact, and with which we are accountable for how we interact. In short: there is what we can sense, but there is also much more. The obvious implications include: existence, personality, design, power, otherness, and beauty. These are attributes we must explain if we are to have a satisfying worldview.

In our sensory experience, when we see systems come to exist at the hands of people, we reason that they all have common characteristics: (1) they are all designed intentionally, (2) they are made by someone, (3) they all serve a purpose, and (4) they can be functional or broken. From an innate awareness, we assume the same thing of the natural systems we observe. There was intentional design, by a Designer, for a purpose, and the design may or not be working. With emotion, we are struck by the significance of the implications, and with desire and will we want to know more of this design and Designer – both on a cognitive and personal level.

To consider that there is a design, a designer, purpose, and functionality initially satisfies reason, provides explanatory value for experienced phenomena, and implies a potentially discernible meaning. To deny any of these four implications would be to put remarkable strain on credulity, based on our application of the tools so far. There is, of course, need for further explanation than simply these generalities in order to ultimately satisfy the three questions, so the quest is not done, but it has begun. But we can go little further than these first rudimentary steps with the five tools, as their scope is limited. (Incidentally, the acknowledgment of limitation is not a call for the discontinued use of the five tools in the pursuit of truth, just a recognition that there is something more needed.) Natural or general revelation has introduced us to God. We sense, reason, and intuit through what has been made that He is, and some significant aspects of who He is.

The Ultimate Tool

After initial assessment of our own data, we begin to assess the data of others, through their tools. We consider writings of science and history, and recognize that there is value in the thoughts of others, but we are still looking for something more broadly explanatory and reliable. At this point, we open the Bible. Initially, we read it simply as a source of information. we know nothing yet of inspiration, inerrancy, or infallibility. We are simply reading. We discover in its pages that the book affirms the five tools, the three questions, even the challenges, and ultimately provides answers to the three great questions of worldview.

The book affirms that we have reason and are supposed to use it (Is 1:18, Rom 12:3), that the senses are useful tools (1 Cor 12:16-18), that emotion is an important part of personality (e.g., the Psalms), that desire and will can be good sources of initiative (2 Thes 1:11, 1 Tim 3:1), and that there is an innate awareness of reality, truth, and God (Ecc 3:11, Rom 1:19). The book also affirms that reason is limited (Rom 1:22), the senses can deceive (Gen 27, Jer 17:9), emotions can get out of hand (Prov 14:29-30), desire and will can be misplaced (Jam 4:1-5), and conscience can be violated (1 Tim 4:2). *The Bible affirms both the usefulness of the five tools and their limitations.* The implication is clear: it is with caution that one should rely on these tools in forming a worldview, yet, they are ours and with purpose.

Still, the Bible offers itself as a sixth, and fully authoritative tool. Proverbs 1:7 and 9:10 describe the fear of the Lord essentially as the beginning of knowledge, wisdom, and understanding. Further, the assertion is that the fear of the Lord is ascertained through the word of God (Prov 2:6), and there are many internal implications and claims that the content of the Bible is the word of God (e.g., Mt 14:13, Lk 11:51, 16:16, 24:44, Rom 3:21, 2 Tim 3:16, Rev 22:16-18). The Bible makes the claim of being unlimited where the other five tools are limited. In particular (for this context), the Bible addresses the three great questions of satisfying reason, explaining experience, and ascertaining meaning.

The Bible claims to offer the path for the proper use of reason, offering a superior wisdom (1 Cor 1:21-31, 2:10-16, Jam 3:13-18) and a comprehensive epistemology. It presents an explanatory model, accounting for human experience and a robust metaphysic (Prov 3:19-20, 4:20-27, Lk 24:27, Jn 1:18, Acts 11:4, 17:3, Col 2:2-3). Finally, the Bible claims to be a road map for purpose and meaning in life (Ecc 1-12, Jn 17:3, Jn 20:30-31, Rom 12:1-2) with well-grounded ethics and socio-political implications.

But can we trust the Bible as a legitimate and reliable source? Let's return to the five tools: reason, the senses, emotion, will, and innate awareness. The Bible as an authentic and authoritative source satisfies intellectual consideration in at least five ways. (1) In comparison to other works of antiquity, the manuscript evidence for the authenticity of the Bible far exceeds any other. While there are certainly variants between different manuscripts of the same passages, the variants ore most often very, very minor, and do not typically impact the meaning. (2) The relatively small number and degree of variants is an evidence for careful transmission of the text, and a reliable process that largely has been faithful in preserving the text. (3) The unity and continuity of narrative and themes of the Bible is more indicative of a central authorship than simply a collection of generally related books. The Biblical themes are tightly wound and consistently presented throughout. Further, (4) there is a traceable higher criticism pedigree connecting each book – there is not just unity in the narrative, but there is a viable connectedness in authorship, all centrally revolving around the person of Jesus (we will get back to Him in a moment). Finally, (5) the amount of prophecy fulfilled and the detail of those fulfillments are at least curious if not utterly convincing.

The Bible does appeal to the senses in light of its authenticity. One writer appeals to the reader to "taste and see that the Lord is good" (Ps 34:8). In that sense one might recommend the Scriptures, suggesting that they are "sweeter than honey" (Ps 19:10), and that the ways therein are pleasant, peaceful, and bring happiness (Prov 3:17-18).

The Bible presents itself as soothing to the emotions. It is to be treasured, brings joy, and gives occasion for delight. It presents itself as an object of desire (Prov 3:15). Finally, it

IMPLICATIONS OF PRIORITY   243

presents itself as true, appealing to an innate awareness that it is indeed true (Ecc 3:11, 1 Jn 2:20-21, c.f., Ps 14:1).

Ultimately, though, the question is a historical and personal one revolving around the person of Jesus Christ. He is recorded as having asked the greatest question in Matthew 16:15: "Who do you say that I am?" That is the question we all must answer. If He is who He is recorded to be, then He is the Creator who brought the cosmos into existence. As such He has the rights of ownership and it is fitting that all His creation should be accountable to Him. If He is who He is recorded to be, then He provides the greatest evidence for the Bible's authenticity. He acknowledged the veracity of the Hebrew Bible (Lk 11:51, 24:44), and He commissioned His followers to bear witness of Him (Jn 15:26, 16:13, Acts 9:15) – many of them did so in the writings of the Greek New Testament, in a process Peter describes in some detail (2 Pet 1:20-21). If He is who He is recorded to be, then the Bible is worthy of our reliance as the epistemological basis of our worldview, and as the source for the rest of our worldview as well. If the Bible is right on this one point (the identity of Jesus Christ), then it is trustworthy on all.

As we taste and discover that the Lord is indeed good, we continue to appreciate the Bible, finding it intellectually satisfying, sufficiently explanatory of experience, and fitting the needs and designs of emotion, will, and conscience. The Bible addresses great questions of life in a coherent way that corresponds to what we observe through experience in reality. It does so in a way that soothes emotion, will, and conscience by providing clear meaning and purpose.

We find that the Bible does not at all inhibit learning and discovery, rather it is the slingshot that propels us to seek and discover what He has done and who He is. It is the very catalyst for our pursuit of a truth and meaning. It informs disciplines of study, it does not obfuscate them. At the core of any worldview is its basis for truth, knowledge, and certainty. The Bible provides an elegant, wondrous basis, setting our courses of study with joy and purpose. The Bible guides and oversees the other tools we have been given, so that we are not without help along the way. He is, He always was, and He always will be. And He revealed Himself first through His cosmos (Gen 1, Rom 1), then through His word (2 Tim 3:16), and ultimately through His Son (Jn 1:18, Heb 1:1-2). We can know Him (Jn 17:3), and walk with Him (Jn 15:4). Ultimately, *that* is what the Biblical worldview is all about.

As God's word brings us a much more detailed knowledge of our Creator (2 Tim 3:16-17, 2 Pet 1:20-21), we learn through this word of our failure (Rom 3:23), our separation from Him (Eph 2:3, 12), and our need for Him (Jn 14:6, 15:5). We learn of His provision of grace and mercy through the death of Jesus Christ for our sins (Rom 1:16-17, 3:21-25, 1 Cor 15: 3-4, Eph 2:4-6), and we learn of how, by belief in Him, we can have eternal life (Jn 3:16, 6:47) and become children of God (Jn 1:12), as evidenced by the power of Jesus' own resurrection from the dead (Jn 11:25, Rom 1:4, 1 Cor 15:20). We learn of the richness of our position in Christ (Eph 1:3), the power and security of the Holy Spirit in our lives (Eph 1:13-14, 1 Cor 12:7, 13), the provision of brothers and sisters who are to love and encourage us and to whom we are to do the same (1 Cor 12:12, Col 3:16-17, Heb 10:24, 1 Jn 4:11), and our future inheritance of being face to face with Him once our journey here is through (2 Cor 5:8, 1 Thes 4:17).

God's word provides the believer with a remarkable certainty that is the absolute birthright of the believer in Jesus Christ. *This is the Biblical worldview.* Yet if we fail to hear and heed God's word because we have disregarded how He intends for us to understand His word, then we have erred greatly. We have not simply made a tactical error with a few minor theoretical implications. We have covered our eyes and ears and are shouting out our own preferences and our own decrees, drowning out the words of life and truth He has so lovingly given us. We declare – as if we are somehow entitled to such authority – our own worldview, rooted in an epistemology we have shaped, promoting a metaphysic we have created, following an ethics after our own desires, and preaching a socio-political model for our own conveniences. We miss who He reveals Himself to be. We miss the sweetness of getting to know Him – the very meaning of our lives (Jn 17:3). We miss the joy of doing life as He designed (Eph 2:10). We miss the beautiful task He has given us to do with a beyond-the-sun perspective (Ecc 12:13). We miss how He intends us to interact with each other.

Ultimately, if we fall into this error we are no longer tasting and seeing that the Lord is good (Ps 34:8). We are trading that most wondrous flavor for something far inferior and for something fully inauthentic. Herein is the priority of Biblical hermeneutics and theological method: that we hear our Creator *as He has spoken*, and that we respond as He has designed, for our highest benefit (2 Tim 3:16-17), and – much more importantly – to the praise of His glory (Rom 11:33-36).

www.ingramcontent.com/pod-product-compliance
Lightning Source LLC
Chambersburg PA
CBHW070141100426
42743CB00013B/2783